RIVERS AND RIVERINE LANDSCAPE
IN
NORTH EAST INDIA

About the Editors

Dr. S. Sengupta is a senior faculty in Geography in St. Mary's College, Shillong. She has edited a book entitled *Shillong — A Tribal City in Transition* published in 2004. Also, she has to her credit several research articles published in different volumes. She has presented as well papers on pupulation studies, economic and regional studies in many national and international seminars, workshops and conferences.

Dr. K.R. Sinha is a senior lecturer in the Department of Geography, St. Mary's College, Shillong. Her field of specialization is agricultural geography and agricultural policies. Currently, she is working as the Director in a UGC sponsored project on "Geo-Environment Appraisal of Shillong Urban Agglomeration with Special Reference to Solid Waste Management."

Ms. S. Purkayastha, lecturer in Geography, St. Mary's College, Shillong, has registered as a research scholar in North Eastern Hill University. Her field of specialization is Geomorphology. She has undertaken research on geo-environmental issues of Shillong town. Also, she is one of the joint coordinators of the UGC sponsored project on "Geo-Environment Appraisal of Shillong Urban Agglomeration with Special Reference to Solid Waste Management".

Ms. W.B. Rani, lecturer in Geography, St. Mary's College, Shillong, is also a joint coordinator of the UGC sponsored Project on "Geo-Environment Appraisal of Shillong Urban Agglomeration with Special Reference to Solid Waste Management".

Ms. S. Das, lecturer in Geography, St. Mary's College, Shillong, has to her credit a good number of research articles published in books and periodicals. She has presented papers in many regional, national and international seminars, workshops and conferences. She takes particular interest in urban social studies.

RIVERS AND RIVERINE LANDSCAPE IN NORTH EAST INDIA

Editors
S. SENGUPTA, K.R. SINHA
S. DAS, W.B. RANI
S. PURKAYSTHA

CONCEPT PUBLISHING COMPANY, NEW DELHI-110059

Cataloging in Publication Data—DK
Courtesy: D.K. Agencies (P) Ltd. <docinfo@dkagencies.com>

Rivers and riverine landscape in North East India /
editors, S. Sengupta ... [et al.].
p. cm.
Papers presented at a seminar.
Includes bibliographical references.
Includes index.
ISBN 8180692760

1. Rivers—India, Northeastern—Congresses. 2. Stream ecology—India, Northeastern—Case studies—Congresses. 3. Valleys—India, Northeastern—Congresses. I. Sengupta, Sutapa, 1955-

DDC 551.483 095 41 22

ISBN-81-8069-276-0

First Published 2006

Published and Printed by
Ashok Kumar Mittal
Concept Publishing Company
A/15-16, Commercial Block, Mohan Garden
New Delhi-110059 (India)

Phones : 25351460, 25351794
Fax : 091-11-25357103
E-mail : publishing@conceptpub.com

PREFACE

The North Eastern Region of India is a land of rivers. Rivers like Brahmaputra, Barak and their numerous tributaries drain the entire region. These major and minor rivers and their innumerable tributaries in the region determine primarily the natural vegetation, soil composition, fertility and expanse of cultivable land and in turn also have considerable impact on the settlement patterns of human groups and their preference for farming practices. Presence or absence of rivers is also significant from the view point of generation of hydroelectricity, development of inland navigation, possibilities of irrigation and so on. Further the rivers in the region have been the root cause of one of the pertinent natural calamities, that is, flood and annual inundation of their basin areas. Thus, controlling of flood and soil erosion remains as one of the major developmental programmes in the region for which a proper understanding of hydraulics of the stream flow is essential. The river systems in the North Eastern Region of India are, thus, significant in almost every sphere of life whether physical, economic or socio-cultural.

The present discussion intends to focus on these above mentioned issues which are closely linked with the rivers in any region. In the context of North-East India, such a discussion is even more significant since most of the region's rivers are interregional and some are even international, which make the study and management of the rivers far more complex. The present project undertakes to study the river systems in the region as a whole and the cases of particular rivers along with their overall impact on the natural landscape, rural and urban morphology and regional development.

The discussion made in the present book has been divided into two parts preceded by a general introduction given by Mohammed Taher. In his keynote address, Taher dealt at length on the works of the major and minor river systems of the region and brought out the existing and potential development programmes linked with these river systems.

The first part of the book deals with the various problems, prospects of the north eastern rivers and progresses made by them in the physical and socio-cultural aspects of the region. While Mohapatra attempted a theoretical and methodological framework for the decision-making processes regarding the preservation, conservation and regeneration of river systems; Goswami and Choudhury together dealt with the existing scenario of hydropower development. They have also suggested some positive measures for enhancing the status of the existing projects.

The second part of the book deals with the discussion of the individual rivers and some of their tributaries. The first four papers deal particularly with the mighty Brahmaputra and some of its tributaries. Highlighting the historical, physical, cultural and economic significances of the river Brahmaputra, Bora has pointed out a need for proper planning of the water to generate hydro-electricity and use for irrigation, which otherwise is wasted every year into he basin area of the river.

Saikia and Das together have discussed the role of river Brahmaputra on inland water transport system and thus have highlighted the role of river on the economic development of this river valley in particular and that of the region at large. Nath made her discussion on the impact of irrigation projects developed from Jia-Dhansiri, one of the largest tributaries of Brahmaputra. She has pointed out the changing status of agricultural development in Darrang district of Assam, which is primarily dependent on this irrigation project.

The last of these four paper deals with the physical and cultural landscape in one of the major confluence zones of Brahmaputra valley. Gogoi has made a very interesting attempt in this line taking the case of Lohit, Dibang and Dihang confluence zone.

Four scholars have made the deliberation on the streams of Shillong and Shillong region at length. While Gupta has highlighted the geological, biological and ecological aspects of the streams of Shillong region along with the biodiversity in the stream basin areas; Subrata Purkayastha and Susmita Das have together discussed the impact of river channels and river slopes on the urban growth and urbanization of Shillong at different time periods. The case of river Umaiam in Meghalaya has been discussed by Uttama Choudhury, dealing particularly with the impact of the river on the industrial growth and development in Meghalaya.

The geomorphological characteristic of the Imphal river basin and its impact on the development of the valley has been discussed by Bandyopadhyay, which according to him depends on the behavioural pattern of the river itself.

The ecological-agricultural condition of the Barak valley in Assam has been attempted together by Choudhury and Dutta. Taking into consideration the fluctuation in the river regime of the Barak (in the forms of flood and drought), they have highlighted the behavioural pattern and preferences of farmers in the valley in terms of choice of growing of particular varieties of rice crop.

The behavioural pattern of rivers of North Bengal, a region very close to the North East India, has been discussed by Jana, who has also highlighted the impact of these rivers on the development of the region. The book ends with an account of a few brief notes being related with the theme of the project.

The completion of the book has taken place in several stages. Initially, a seminar was held on the theme : "River Systems in the North Eastern India and their Impact upon the Region's Environmental Development". A few selected papers presented in the seminar were then edited thoroughly and compiled for publication.

The editors of the book are indebted to Concept Publishing Company, who has undertaken the responsibility of publishing the book. We are also grateful to a number of organizations and institutions who had provided financial help, without which carrying out and completion of the project would have been impossible. We received financial grants from the NER center of University Grants Commission, Guwahati; Government of Meghalaya; The Meghalaya Cooperative Apex Bank, Shillong; Indian Council of Social Science

Research (ICSSR), New Delhi; ICSSR, North Eastern Regional Council Shillong; North East Electrical Power Corporation (NEEPCO), Shillong. We put on record our sincere gratitude for them. We also take this opportunity to thank our reverend principal Dr. (Sr.) Philomena Kharakor, whose dynamic personality has remained a constant source of inspiration at each and every stage of the project.

Last, but not least, we also put on record our gratefulness to Dr. Basudev Datta Ray, Secretary, North East India Council of Social Science Research, Shillong, who gave the most valuable advice as and when we needed them.

Though quite a long time has lapsed between holding the seminar and publishing the proceedings, but, since the deliberations are related to mcre or less permanent landscapes of the regions, we hope the volume still has relevance in understanding the environmental situations of the region.

Shillong **Editors**

CONTENTS

LIST OF CONTRIBUTORS

Bandyopadhyay, M. K.
Professor, Department of Geography,
Calcutta University, Kolkata

Bora, Ashok Kumar
Reader, Department of Geography,
Gauhati University, Guwahati

Choudhury, Aparajit
Assistant Manager (c) P & D NEEPCO Ltd.
Shillong

Choudhury, Dhrupad
Reader, Department of Life Sciences,
Assam University, Silchar

Choudhury, Uttama
North Eastern Hill University,
Shillong

Das, Prabhat
ACS, Hailakandi, Assam

Das, Susmita
Lecturer, Department of Geography,
St. Mary's College, Shillong

Dutta, Jibendu
Department of Zoology,
M.H.C. College of Science and Technology, Silchar

Gogoi, Bhuban
Lecturer, Tinsukia College,
Tinsukia, Assam

Goswami, Monomoy
Assistant Manager (c) P & D NEEPCO Ltd.
Shillong

Gupta, Abhik
Reader, Department of Ecology,
Assam University, Silchar

Jana, M. M.
Professor, Department of Geography and Applied Geography,
University of North Bengal,
Darjeeling

Mohapatra, A. C.
Professor , Department of Geography,
North Eastern Hill University,
Shillong

Purkayastha, Subrata
Lecturer, Department of Geography, St. Mary's College,
Shillong

Saharia, N. Charu
Lecturer, Department of Geography,
Tezpur College,
Tezpur, Assam

Saikia, Bhupen
Lecturer, Department of Geography,
Tezpur College, Tezpur, Assam

Taher, Mohmmed
Professor, Emeritus, Department of Geography,
Gauhati University, Guwahati

LIST OF FIGURES

LIST OF TABLES

INTRODUCTION

MOHAMMED TAHER

KEYNOTE SPEECH

Honourable President, esteemed scholars, revered colleagues, ladies and gentlemen present. I feel extrememly honoured on being called upon to deliver the keynote speech on this very important topic before this august gathering of the luminaries. However, I shall make a brief speech by way of giving a geographical introduction to the river system of the North East India and the status of the environment in which they exist.

North East India falls within the tropical monsoon climate with an average annual rainfall of 200 cm. It may be noted that the region contains the rainiest locality of the world, i.e. the Mawsynram - Cherrapunjee area. Besides, North East India has one of the densiest drainage network in the world, due essentially to high rainfall and the character of the topography with hills, mountain and flat land just opposed together. There are seven sets of drainage system covering the region. They are (i) the Brahmaputra in the north, (ii) Barak - surma system in the middle, (iii) Chindwin system fed by the Tizu, Yu and Manipur rivers in the east and south-east, (iv) Chimtuipui in the southern part, (v) Karnaphuli in the western part of Mizoram (vi) Gumti in the middle part and (vii) Feni in the southern part of Tripura. All these systems are international in their extension and go either to Bangladesh or Myanmar. Of these seven systems, the Brahmaputra and Barak system are very much extensive, the other five are small, but large or small of all the river systems cut across the international boundary, thus assuming environmental and strategic importance. For a vivid picture the systems are discussed below individually.

The Brahmaputra System

The Brahmaputra, one of the largest river of the world has 920 km lying within North East India out of its total length 2880 km, the basin of the Brahmaputra within North East India covers 165000 km^2, including whole of Arunachal Pradesh and major parts of Assam, Nagaland and Meghalaya, accounting for 70 per cent of the total area of the region.

The tsangpo, the main head stream of the Brahmaputra, enters into North East India at Kepang la above Tuting, after its long 1700 km of travel over the Tibetan plateau. Here its bed is at an altitude of 3600 m a.s.l. and is full of cascades and cataracts. The river here takes the name of Siang and flows through a highly mountainous country for 200 km through deep gorges and waterfall, until it reaches Pasighat at the southern Himalayan foothills, at an altitude of 350 m. The river in this mountainous course receives several tributaries both on its left and right banks. The average gradient of the river here is 17 m/km. On entering the plain it takes the name of Dihang and meets with Dihong and Lohit, two equally large rivers, and create an extensively low lying flat topography criss-crossed braided channels. From this tri-junction the river takes the name Brahmaputra and begins to flow south-westward for about 150 km upto Dihingmukh and then slowly takes westward course for about 500 km until it reaches Dhubri.Near Dhubri, Brahmaputra takes a sudden southerly turn and flows for about 40 km. before entering Bangladesh.

From its tri-junction near Kobo to Mankachar, where it leaves North East India, the river receives as many as 104 large and small tributaries of which Jia, Dhul, Subansiri, Ranganadi, Dikrong, Buroi, Bargang, Jia Bharali, Gabharu, Jia Dhansiri, Barnadi, Pagladia, Beki, Manas, Champamati, Godadhar and Sankosh, in the north-bank and Dibru, Burhi Dihin, Disang, Dikhou, Janji, Kakadonga, Kopili, Digaru, Kulsi, Dudhnoi, Krishnai and Jinjiram of the south-bank are the main. While the main catchment areas of the north-bank tributries fall with in Arunachal Himalaya, those of the south-bank tributaries are over Nagaland, North Cachar Hills and the Meghalaya Plateau. The catchment areas of several of these rivers are above 5000 km^2 each. All these tributaries, apart from the main headstreams of Dihang, Dibang and Lohit, carry down million of tonnes of sediments and spread these over not only the beds of the rivers themselves, but also on the flat Brahmaputra plain, especially during the period of heavy monsoon rainfall. Brahmaputra carries about 402 m tonnes of sediment on the average annually. This phenomenon reflects itself in a number of topographic consequences. *Firstly,* the Brahmaputra plain has become extremely flat, the gradient between Kobo and Dhubri being hardly 14 cm/km. *Secondly,* the sediments deposited on the bed of the Brahmaputra have given rise to numerous riverine shoals and semi-permanent island rendering the river wide and braided. *Thirdly,* the tributaries themselves, especially the north-bank ones, braid near the foothills and meander sluggishly down-stream. *Fourthly,* in order to accommodate the large volumes of turbulently flowing water in the period of heavy deluge in summer, extensive bank erosion takes place in almost all the rivers including the Brahmaputra. *Fifthly,* the channels of the north-bank tributaries being choked with sediments, often change the course in summer causing immense damage to land and material. *Finally,* there occurs devastating floods in the plain in every rainy season.

To add to the fury of floods, the Brahmaputra has four construction in its bed within North East India. The first construction at Mahmara Gaon South West of Kobo, the second one is near Silghat, the third one is between Guwahati and North Guwahati and the last one is between Pancharatna and Jogijhopa. The river channel in these places are relatively narrow, hindering a regular flow of rain and snow-melt water in summer, making their upstream areas vulnerable to flooding.

The topography of the Brahmaputra basın is made of high Himalayan mountains reaching an altitude above 6000 m, the Lesser Himalayan hills varying in altitude between 300 m and 400 m and the flat Brahmaputra Plain located at 40 m to 300 m.

The Barak System

The Barak system of rivers lies in the middle part of North East India covering an area of about 52,000 km^2. The river Barak originates at the border of Nagaland and Manipur, east of Mao and flows westward for some distance forming the boundary between Nagaland and Manipur and then suddenly turns southward and flows through Manipur until it reaches Tipaimukh, south of the tri-junction of Assam, Manipur and Mizoram. Then it takes a northward turn, flows for about 60 km and turns westward at Jirimukh and runs through the Cachar Plain sluggishly. Near Karimganj it bifurcates into the northern branch of Surma and the southern branch of Kushiyara.

The drainage basin of the Barak covers the northern and western parts of Manipur, southern parts of North Cachar Hills and Meghalaya, the plain districts of Cachar, Karimganj and Hailakandi and the northern parts of Mizoram and Tripura. The Barak has a length of 525 km within North East India. Of this, about 400 km of its course is hilly where it falls from a height of about 2000 m to about 150 m and the remaining 125 km is over the Cachar plain over which it flows through a sluggish course. Its important right-bank tributaries include Makru and Jiri in Manipur and Labak, Modhura, Dalu, Jatinga and Larang in the Cachar plain. The major left-bank tributaries are Irong and Tuivai (Tipai) in Manipur and Sonai, Rukni, Katakhal, Daleswari, Singla and Longai in the plains. Besides, several tributaries from northern Tripura falls into its Kushiyara branch in Bangladesh. Similarly, Lubha, Kangs, Jadukata and Someswari fall into its northern branch i.e., Surma in the Bangladesh Plain.

The Barak has its bed graded even inside Manipur hills upto about 150 km upstream from Jiribam (where it enters the plain). Hence, country boats can ply deep into Manipur and Mizoram hills along this river. Over the Cachar Plain, the river has an extremely meandering course, rendering wide areas on both of its banks swampy flood plains gagged with ox-bow lakes.

The Chindwin Drainage System

Although the Chindwin River flows within Mynmar, a large number of its headstreams drain the eastern part of North East India, especially the areas bordering that country. The three important tributaries through which this drainage has been set up are the Tizu, Yu and Manipur rivers. The Tizu drains the south eastern part of Nagaland and north eastern part of Manipur and then falls into the Chindwin. The Yu with its headstreams drains the eastern margin of Manipur and then flows south meeting the Chindwin finally. The Manipur River sub-basin is more important in that it drains the central and southern parts of Manipur including the lowlying Manipur Basin. The tributaries, Imphal, Iril and Thoubal, which originate in the Hills of the North Central part of the State, flow south, descend to the Basin and meet one another south of the Imphal City. The combined water course takes the name of Turel Achouba or Manipur River or Imphal River and flows south by the eastern side of the Loktak Lake and leaves North East India to meet Myittha, a tributary of Chindwin in Mynmar. Near Loktak it is joined to the lake by a channel called Khuga. The area in North East India under the drainage system of Chindwin covers about 24,000 km^2. While the rivers Tizu and Yu still retain steep hilly character, the main headstream of Manipur River, viz., Iril, Imphal and Thoubal have graded course over the Basin, causing heavy siltation and assuming meandering courses. The siltation so caused has recently led to shrinking of the Loktak Lake and other low lying areas of the Basin.

The Chimtuipui System

The river Kaladan or Chimtuipui has set up its drainage basin over the southern and south-east part of Mizoram in the Lunglei and Chimtuipui districts. Its important tributary is Mangpui Lui. In the central eastern part of Mizoram, its another tributary, Tuichong, drains a part of Champhai sub-division. The drainage basin of Chimtuipui covers an area of about 7000 km^2. It flows due south to Mynmar across the southern boundary of Mizoram in the name of Kaladan and falls into the Bay of Bengal.

The Karnaphuli System

Although the Karnaphuli is an important river of the south-eastern part of Bangladesh, almost all of its headstreams lie on the western margin of Mizoram. The important ones among them are Phairang, Tuichong, Thega, Doh and Tuiliangpui. They meet one another near Demagiri and flows south-east to Bangladesh in the name of Karanphuli. The drainage area of this river in North East India is about 4000 km^2.

The Gumti System

Gumti is an important river of the middle part of Tripura draining a large part of West Tripura district and a small part of South Tripura district. The Gumti ultimately falls into Meghna and has about 2500 km^2 of drainage basin in North East India.

The Feni System

The Feni is a small river, which along with its headstreams, drains the major part of South Tripura district. Its basin in North East India accounts for an area of about 1500 km^2.

Perspective on Development

We have got a geographical introduction to the river system of North East India. Although there is an overall environmental homogeneity among all the river basins, there are certain differences in the high Himalayan part of the Brahmaputra Basin from the rest because of its altitude cause variation in climatic and geomorphological process. Besides, the hills and mountains on the one hand, and plains on the other, have differences in respect of both environment and human activities. These variations call for an independent assessment of each of the river basin areas. A cursory glance over them reveals the following facts:

The Brahmaputra Basin

This basin of about 1,65,000 km^2 area, consists of about 100,000 km^2 of hills and mountains and 65,000 km^2 of low lying plains. Total population in this basins is about 22.9 million. Although, average density turns out to be about 10 km^2, there are 3 density zones, the Brahmaputra Plain having density of 350 persons/km^2 followed by the Arunachal, Nagaland and Meghalaya foot hills with density ranging between 30 to 70 km^2 and the high Himalayan area where density drops down to less than 6 person/km^2. The area has land, forest, water and mineral resources and hence there have come up 102 towns of different sizes. The region has the problems of drainage, flood, landslide in the hills and lack of infrastructural development including underdeveloped transport and communication. The towns mentioned above may be taken as growth centres and growth points for prospective development.

The Barak Basin

Of the 52,000 km^2 of the area of Barak drainage system, only about 9,000 km^2 is plain while the remaining 43,000 km^2 is hilly. The total population of this basin is about 4.55 million, accounting for an overall density of 88/km^2, but it has a 3 tier distribution, while the Manipur hills within the basin has a density of only 20/km^2, the Mizoram, Meghalaya and Tripura Hills have about 50-60 persons/km^2 and the Barak plain has to support about 400 souls/km^2. Resources of the region include land, forest, water and natural gas, coal and limestone. The basin has 27 small and big towns. The problems include flood in the plain, landslide in the hills, isolation and lack of development of transport and communication.

The Chindwin Drainage Basin

This drainage system containing high hill ranges in the eastern margin of North East India spreads over 24,000 km^2 with only about 2200 km^2 of plain land represented by the Manipur Basin.

The total population of the drainage is 1.6 million accounting for an average density of 67 persons/km^2. But here again there is distributional disparity. While the Phek and Tuensang districts of eastern Nagaland has a density of 50/km^2, the eastern Manipur or Yu Sub-basin has a density of only 20 persons/km^2 but Manipur Basin has the highest density in North East India with more than 400 persons/km^2. The resources of the region include land, water, forest and many varieties of minerals yet to be fully explored. There are 27 towns, large and small, which can act as growth points for regional economic development. The problems are of landslides in the hills, flood and poor drainage in the plains, isolation and lack of development of transport and communication.

The Chimtuipui System

The whole of the 7,000 km^2 of this basin is hilly, although hills are not as high as in the case of the previous basin. The total population of this basin is about 1.5 lakhs with an average density of 25-30 persons/km^2. The resources include land, water and forest. There are 9 towns in this region which have come up as administrative and service centres of Mizoram. This basin area is one of the most isolated in whole of India with extremely poor development of transport and communication.

The Karnaphuli System

It is a small basin with an area of 4000 km^2 and a population of 25,000 in Lunglei district. Average density is 25 persons/km^2. Land, forest and water are its resources. The only town worth the name is Tlabung or Demagiri which must be developed as the launching pad of development of the region. Like the above area, this area is also handicapped with isolation, in spite of it being strategically important.

The Gumti Drainage System

Gumti basin covers the densely populated West Tripura district and the marginal areas of Dholai and South Tripura districts (area:

2500 km^2). It supports a population of 17 lakhs with a density of 370 persons/km^2. The resources of the region include land, water, forest and natural gas. The problems are isolation and underdevelopment. There are 12 towns in this area which can be used as growth points.

The Feni River System

This is the smallest river system covering only 1500 km^2 of the southern part of South Tripura district. It supports about 3 lakh population with an average density of 180-200 persons/km^2. Like other parts, its known resources are land, water and forest. The only town here is Belonia, which holds the potentiality of being an important commercial centre with Bangladesh. The region's problems are the same as other parts of Tripura i.e., isolation and lack of development of transport and communication.

Conclusion

We have had a brief introudction of the river systems of North East India and their physico-economic environment.

Each of the seven river basins holds out potentiality with land, water, forest and to some extent minerals. But each of them is also handicapped with certain physical problems like flood, ill drainage, landslide, etc., and socio-economic problems like poor development of transport and communication and other infrastructures necessary for development.

River basins are often considered as scientific units for regional development, for they provide important clues for development of land, water and forest resources. As such taking the basins as units and accepting the towns (179 of them) as the growth points and centres, the North Eastern Region can be developed well. But for that two things must be achieved. Firstly, development of a solid transport and communication base and secondly, development of human resource in the true sense of the term.

PART-I

GENERAL BACKGROUND

1

VALUING THE RIVER

A. C. MOHAPATRA

In the history and tradition of India, the river plays an overwhelming role — shaping her economy and the culture. All old civilisations were cradled in river valleys. But the importance of a river in a tropical country with a nine-month dry period led to the symbolism of river as the life-giver, the concept of Ganga — the mother and provider. Lately, modern industrialism, population expansion and over-exploitation have caused serious degradation to the country's river systems. Whereas development has brought in benefits, it has also imposed environmental costs, normally not entered in the books of cost-benefit.

The river for the Indian society has been extremely *valuable,* it remains so and will remain more so in the future, for development and sustainability of the civilisation. River provides both *use value* and *non-use values.* The use value is derived out of *direct uses* like in irrigation, drinking water usage or power generation. The *indirect uses* are from maintenance of groundwater, deposition of silts during flooding and maintaining the fertility of the soil, moderation of the micro-climate etc. The *non-use value* is derived in the form of its scenic significance and the religious and cultural importance to the Indian civilisation.

The intention in this paper is to provide a theoretical and methodological foundation to valuing the river in all its tangibles and intangibles. This is likely to help in evaluating projects as well as in decision-making about social investments in their preservation, conservation and wherever necessary, in re-generation of the river systems.

River is valuable. Human civilisation emerged in river valley. Majority of cities, whether ancient or modern, developed on banks of rivers. Rivers shaped the landscape, created fertile valleys and deltas; they provided sweet water to drink and irrigate the fields of the farmer; provided fish as a vital food; provided a place to live in the densely populated deltas of Yang-tze; in ancient times, they were the highways of transportation and commerce — no less now, — in nut-shell, rivers have been invaluable to human society, its culture, civilisation and economy. It is inconceivable to think of civilisation without the central role that the river played in it. In tropical countries like India, China, or Egypt (the old world civilisations), rivers are even more relevant. It is not far to see why the people assigned divinity to river in India — the eternal mother and the giver of life.

Societies assigned value to rivers both by intuitive reasoning as well as through empirical reasoning. Intuition provided the aesthetic and spiritual values (the intangibles), empirical, the mundane economic and other beneficial values. It is also to be appreciated that with the beginning of the industrial era, the rivers are no more the rivers they were — no more the pristine ambiance nor the sweet-scented water that quenched thirst of millions and billions of humans and other life-forms on earth, for ages. Acute pollution of rivers throughout the world, is a question for survival of man and his civilisation. There is excess drawal of water for a variety of uses, their channels dammed time and again for power and irrigation, their banks constricted by embankments, the water is poisoned and has turned toxic — no more the fish and foul frolic on their blue expanses. This has not ended. Man's needs are unending. Every now and then new project come up. It is there, that the cost-benefits of the project has to take account of the tangible and intangible values of the river in their cost calculus — if the goal is preservation of a sustainable river system for ourselves and for the posterity.

Valuing Benefits and Costs

Rivers are of many benefits and these benefits theoretically can be assigned economic value. However, in practice it is not as easy. Environmental economics provides certain valuation methods and techniques for valuing environmental resources. The river is one. Benefits of river can be in terms of both *direct use values* and *indirect use value.* Direct use value can arise in the form of estimable financial flows of benefits, say from a hydro-electric project or an irrigation project where the society (consumers) purchase the benefits by way of direct financial transactions.[1] The same may apply to fishing in the river that the riparian villagers may use the river as a common property resources or the state may impose a royalty on such rights on the users. Similarly, the state could impose a cess or royalty on use of the river for transportation.[2]

The indirect use of value of the river arises out of benefits that accrue that are valuable to the society but cannot be accssed through direct financial means, either by a user charge or a fiscal method. For example, the flooding of the river brings in benefits by way of deposition of silts on the flood plain and enhances fertility of the crop lands. The farmer gets a better harvest. However, it is difficult for the state to impose a cess or a tax on such silts or to estimate the incremental benefits of flooding and silt deposits on the flood plains. Riparian villagers and townsmen draw water from the river for drinking and domestic use that hardly could be taxed, except for large-scale users, like industries or water purification systems that supply to big cities and receive user charges — that come under the category of direct use value.

The non-use value of a river may be in terms of its *option value* or *existence values.* The river as a resource may not have a use value to day because of its difficult location and current difficulties in harnessing it for whatever economic or non-economic reasons. However, it may hold a potential option value in the future. There also could be trade-offs between the present uses and the future uses. On the other hand, the river may contain some biological diversity whose full benefits are not known today but, could be valuable in future that construct another form of option value. The river may have an existence value — that the society assigns significance to the sheer presence of the river, say Ganga. The society is also ready to spend money to keep the river flowing and in good condition for its cultural or religious significance or for posterity unless the river dies or changes course wholly outside the realm of efforts of the society. These are intangibles. The river has its scenic and leisure potentials that have both use value as well as existence value[3].

The rivers creates some negative values by way of damages it might cause principally due to flooding its banks, damage to crops, live-stocks, residences and lives of people, and wild-life etc. These arise out of purely natural causes and also due to anthropogenic reasons. The anthropogenic costs could be way of habitations and embankments on the levee that block the natural flooding; the pollution of river water by industries and agriculture — the waste water flowing into the river system that causes health costs on the users, loss of fish and biotic life etc. It is difficult to see that man can anyway blame nature and put a cost on such damages. However, man can change in the way it interacts with nature and therefore reduce damages arising out of anthropogenic costs. Some of the damages caused by the river can be mitigated by human action and that has a cost — *damage mitigation costs.* These could be brought into the overall cost calculus of the river.

In general, therefore, the balance of the benefits and costs of the river, in principle gives some idea about the value of the river. Thus, if the value of the river is V_a, then :

$$V_a = V_b - V_c \qquad ...(1)$$

Whereas V_a *is the value of the river,* V_b *is the benefits of the river and* V_c *is the costs of the river that is imposed on the society. Further,* V_b *is the sum total of all use and non-use values :*

$$V_b = V_{bu} + V_{bnu} \qquad ...(2)$$

Whereas V_{bu} *is the use value benefits (direct + indirect) and* V_{bnu} *is non-use value benefits (option + existence values).*

Similarly, the costs of the river (including the damage mitigation costs) could be in terms of the direct costs of damage, V_{cd} + indirect costs, V_{cnd} (of mitigation costs, V_{cm} + shadow costs or opportunity costs, V_{co}). Thus,

$$V_c = V_{cd} + V_{cm} + V_{co} \quad ...(3)$$

Therefore, V can be re-written,

$$V = V_{bu} + V_{bnu} - (V_{cd} + V_{cm} + V_{co}) \quad ...(4)$$

Methodology of Estimation

The theoretical propositions made, need to be seen in light of the methodologies available for estimation of the value. However, there is no single methodology available for the estimation process as a whole. The direct benefits and costs are relatively easy to estimate, say the hydro-power potential of the river, the irrigation potential and the incremental benefits of irrigation on crop productivity, or for that matter the drinking water or industrial uses of water is an essential input. Similarly, the direct costs due to flood damages to property, crops, livestock and lives of people could also be theoretically estimated in a given watershed (by averages over a period of time). However, it is the indirect benefits and hidden costs that raises real problems of estimation.

The indirect benefits, like, say the silt deposits during flooding, perhaps, could be estimated by the differential yield, i.e., between without silt deposit yields and with silt deposit yields, so also, in estimating the transportation benefits. But, the conditions of estimating the *option value* or *existence value* are much more complex. For example, what is the value of the river Gharial in Sundarbans, or the value of the Ganga Dolphin (at Allahabad)? They construe both future value as bio-diversity whose preservation for future is thought necessary (even if, not fully ascertained) and an existence value, that their sheer presence in the river is desirable. The first could be approached by the preservation cost method[4]. The second, by the Willingness to Pay (WTP) methodology[5], i.e., some people from far and near are ready to pay for seeing the Sundarban Gharial or the Ganga Dolphin — their existence has a value, at least for a section of the (informed) society. In the same way, Ganga has a religious connotation for the Hindus, and many visit Ganga to take a holy dip in the river coming from within the country and abroad — that cost them by way of transportation, stay etc. Thus, the *travel cost method* could be an appropriate methodology for estimating such existence values of the river. The same may apply to the scenic significance of the river or stretches of the river that has or can bė utilised from tourism or other leisure purposes, like the white-water rafting (sports).

Conclusion

Why value the river? — Have not we always valued it? The matter here is puting an economic value to the river. This may at once look mechanical, some what unorthodox, or even a prosaic interpretation of the value to an environmental resource that societies intuitively assigned great signficance both for temporal and spiritual reasons. This methodology can help us in conserving this vital heritage and resource and also to use it in a more effecive and judicious manner in many areas of its application.

First, for purposes of conservation of the river systems appropriate valuation is vital — both in terms of the benefits and the costs that are the cause. For any conservation programme like the Ganga Action Plan it is necessary to know the costs of damages and the costs of abatement of damages[6]. It is to be appreciated that it is not practicable to think that the river can be left full to its pure natural state. It is also utopian to think that a conservation programme can restore the river to its original state — about which we know little or even so, the costs may be prohibitive and unacceptable (to the society). The acceptable state on which the river can be used, yet conserved is in between a state of total damage or the pure natural state of the river.

Fig. 1.1 shows the decision support that valuation of damage costs of the river and damage mitigation costs can provide. Left to its own devices, human actions can lead to immense damage to the river system at an incremental rate on the scale of use (on the *X* axis), in terms of increasing health costs to people due to polluted rivers, flooding due to the catchment deforestation, decreased fish yield and loss of livelihood of the fishermen, and so on. These could be mitigated by incurring costs in conservation that would be initially more beneficial per unit of cost but would decline over additional units, a negative function (abatement cost function).

E is the intersection of the two functions that provides a possible optimal choice, i.e., a trade-of between an acceptable damage profile as well as some conservation measures in restoring the river to a state of repair, a social acceptable state incurring a socially acceptable economic costs of abatement.

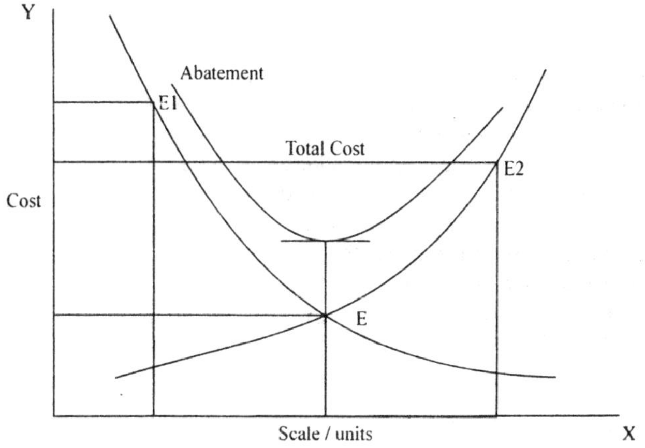

Fig. 1.1 : Environmental Costs and Social Choice

Second, the valuation techniques help in providing resolution of river disputes both internationally as well as nationally. If rivers can be valued, then riparian countries or states can exchange usage of river benefits by trading in rights on their usage[7]. Not far away is the imbroglio of Caurvey, between the states of Tamil Nadu, Karnataka, Kerala and UT of Pondicherry.

Third, the valuation can help in effectively analysing specific development projects, be they of power generation, irrigation, leisure or of drinking water. It may be noted that water itself in such project analysis is treated as a free gift — that in a general sense of true, but looking at increasing scarcity and competing uses, it would be foolhardy to continue with this methodology.

NOTES

1. It may be noted that in project analysis of both hydro-electric type or irrigation type, the cost of water is treated as zero, a free commodity of nature. As a result the (long-term) project costs are either too low or the prices charged are

cost plus basis. This is not a sound methodology under the situation that the water is getting scarce and appropriate pricing may be necessary for the optimal use of the resource. One example is the river water disputes between reparian states (say, the Cauvery dispute). If cost of water as a gift of nature is assigned an economic value (accruing to the reparian states) it is possible that such rights can be traded between countries and/or states and the option will be open whether a particular country or state wishes to utilise the water or wishes to sell it to a down-stream country or state. The result would be much more rewarding and disputes fewer.

2. However, the amount of cess or royalty may not provide a true picture of its value for transportation. This could be estimated by the differential of transport cost with the alternative transportation that is the least cost under the situation.
3. A question may arise about the distinction between the potential benefits and those realise. It could be noted that it is not the intention here to go into this distinction. All realised and potential benefits of the present and future need to be accounted in the framework under discussion.
4. For example, how much would it cost to undertake a preservation programme on the endangered riverine fauna inclusive on educating people, actual conservation programmes and preventive programmes etc.
5. See, Anil Markandya, *The Political Economy of Environment,* Manuscript (Unpublished : 1997).
6. Here the environmental damage cost is confined to anthropogenic costs alone, whereas the abatement costs relate to the mitigation costs that society is to bear to abate or prevent the damage.
7. An interesting parallel is the recenting accepted Global Convention on Climate Change, Kyoto, Japan (December, 1997) in which, negotiating countries agreed on trade in pollution rights distributed among countries, thus encouraging on paying for pollution to countries that are less polluting (the atmosphere).

2

HYDRO POWER POTENTIAL OF THE RIVER SYSTEMS IN THE NORTH EAST : Prospect, Progress and Problem

MONOMOY GOSWAMI and
APARAJIT CHOUDHURY

The enormity of water availability in the rivers of the North East can be gauged by the fact that more than 30 per cent of the annual average of all the rivers of the country is contributed by the Brahmaputra — Barak river system alone which drains the region accounting for about 7.76 per cent of the total geographic area of the country. The availability of this vast natural resource of water, combined with mountainous relief characterised by the mighty Himalayan ranges, has offered great prospect for generation of hydro power in the region, the potential of which is assessed at about 37 per cent of that of the whole country. This paper discusses the prospect of hydro-power development in the North East along with the benefits, both direct and indirect, to be derived from such development. A brief account of the scenario in respect of progress achieved in developing only about 2 per cent of the total hydro potential of the region is included. The hindrances encountered and the problems anticipated in the process of harnessing the water power of the region are highlighted. This has been done with particular reference to some major hydro projects of the region, so that better strategies are evolved in planning for the development of hydro power in the river basins of the region.

INTRODUCTION

Located between 27°57′N and 28°23′N latitude and 89°46′E and 97°25′ E longitudes, the North Eastern (NE) Region of India is situated in the temperate zone of the South Eastern part of Asia and is monsoon blessed. The vast territory of this region is criss-crossed by the river systems of two major basins, namely the Brahamaputra and the Barak, besides some minor ones. These rivers carry, on an average, about 59.07 M ham of water annually to the sea out of a total of 180.16 M ha m assessed for all the rivers in the country. The Siwalik and the north east Himalayan ranges of the mighty Himalayas garland the region and characterise it with huge hydraulic drops. The typical orohydrographical and physiographical combinations render the region a veritable receptacle of enormous hydro power resources. The exploitable hydro potential of the region is 31,857 MW at 60 per cent load factor which is 38 per cent of the total assessed potential of 84,044 MW for the whole of the country and is thus a very significant fraction in projecting India as the seventh ranking nation in terms of exploitable hydro power potential. (Fig. 2.1)

Power is the vital input to any developmental activity and hydro power is a very important source of generation of power. To augment and optimise the power supply to meet the growing need in response to the rapid economic and industrial development in India, a major thrust had been given towards harnessing hydro power resources ever since the era of planned development of the economy was ushered in 1950 and policies and approaches were devised in successive five year plans by giving credence to the realisation of many advantages of hydro power resources over other forms.

The Umtru river, a south-bank tributary of the Brahamaputra, was the first in the NE Region to receive the attention of water power engineers and planners and the genesis of electricity supply industry in the region can be traced back to the commissioning of 8.4 MW Umtru hydro power station in 1957. Although progress had been made in the field of development of hydro power potential of this region since then, yet, from national perspective the extent of about 2.14 per cent potential developed so far in the region, offers a grey area to critically examine the hindrances to such development and suggest remedial measures towards formulating effective hydro power development plans and policies.

The River Systems of the North East

The North Eastern Region of India may be considered as one economically integrated unit served largely by the Brahmaputra-Barak sub-system of the Ganga-Brahmaputra-Meghna system — one of the largest in the world. Besides this, the Manipur river and some other minor river sub-systems such as Kaladan, the Gumti, the Muhuri etc. drain the hills of Manipur, Mizoram, Nagaland and Tripura to flow from the North Eastern Region into Myanmar and Bangladesh. The map showing the river system in the north eastern region is shown in Fig. 2.1.

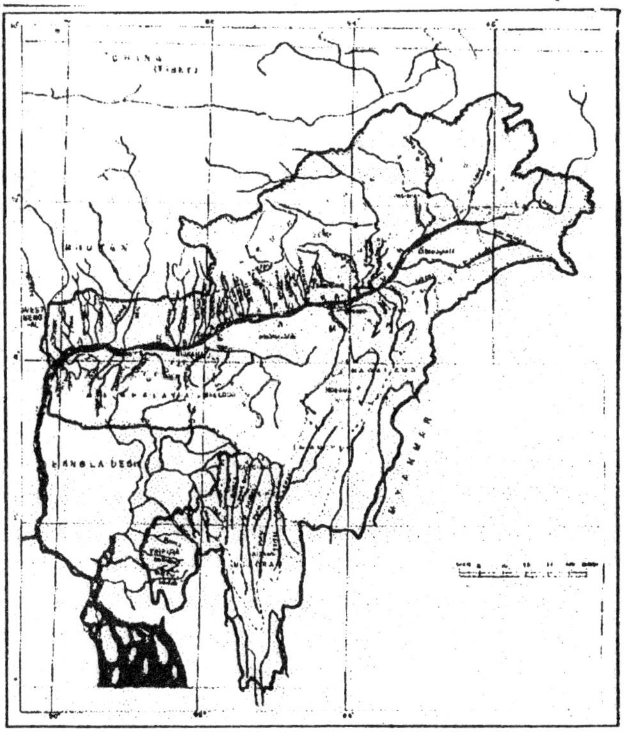

Fig. 2.1 : River System in the North Eastern Region

The Brahmaputra originates in the Kailash Range in the Himalayas. Known as Tsangpo in Tibet, it traverses about 1700 km parallel to the Himalayan mountain ranges in Tibet before entering India in Arunachal Pradesh with a hair pin turn around Namcha Barwa. The river flows down through Arunachal Pradesh in the north east where it is known as the Siang and assumes the name Dihang when entering Assam. After the confluence of the Dihang with the Dibang and the Lohit in Assam, the river is known as the Brahmaputra. In Indian territory, the river flows through some 900 km and receives numerous tributaries on both the north and the south banks. Besides the Dibang and the Lohit the other principal tributaries of the Brahmaputra are the Subansiri, the Kameng, the Dhansiri, the Manas, the Champamati, the Sankosh, the Noa Dihing, the Buri Dihing, the Dishang, the Dikhu and the Dopili. The Brahmaputra enters the alluvial plains of Bangladesh where it flows for about 270 km before joining the Ganga near Goalundo. The tributaries flowing through North Bengal like the Raidak, the Kalyani, the Torsa, the Jalkhaka and the Tista join the mainstream in Bangladesh. In Arunachal Pradesh and Assam, the Brahmaputra has incredibly undercut its bed by some 5500 metres. A significant part of the catchment area of the river in the upper reaches is snowfed. The average annual yield measured at Pandu near Guwahati is around 49 M ham and that reported at Bahadurabad in Bangladesh in around 62.6 M ham. Over three-fourth of this huge volume of water flows during he south-west monsoon season spreading generally from June to October. After November, the flow recedes to an average low flow of 3300 cumec by January-February to rise again thereafter. The peak flows during floods reach magnitudes as high as 71,000 cumec. Figure 2.2 shows the diagrammatic representation of the salient features of the Brahmaputra in the North Eastern Region.

The Barak river, rises in the hills of Manipur in India and flows south-west for some 250 km before it takes a reflex bend and flows north. The river emerges from the hills near Lakhipur in Assam and starts flowing west. At Bhanga, the Barak splits into the Surma and the Kushiyara which cross over into Bangladesh near

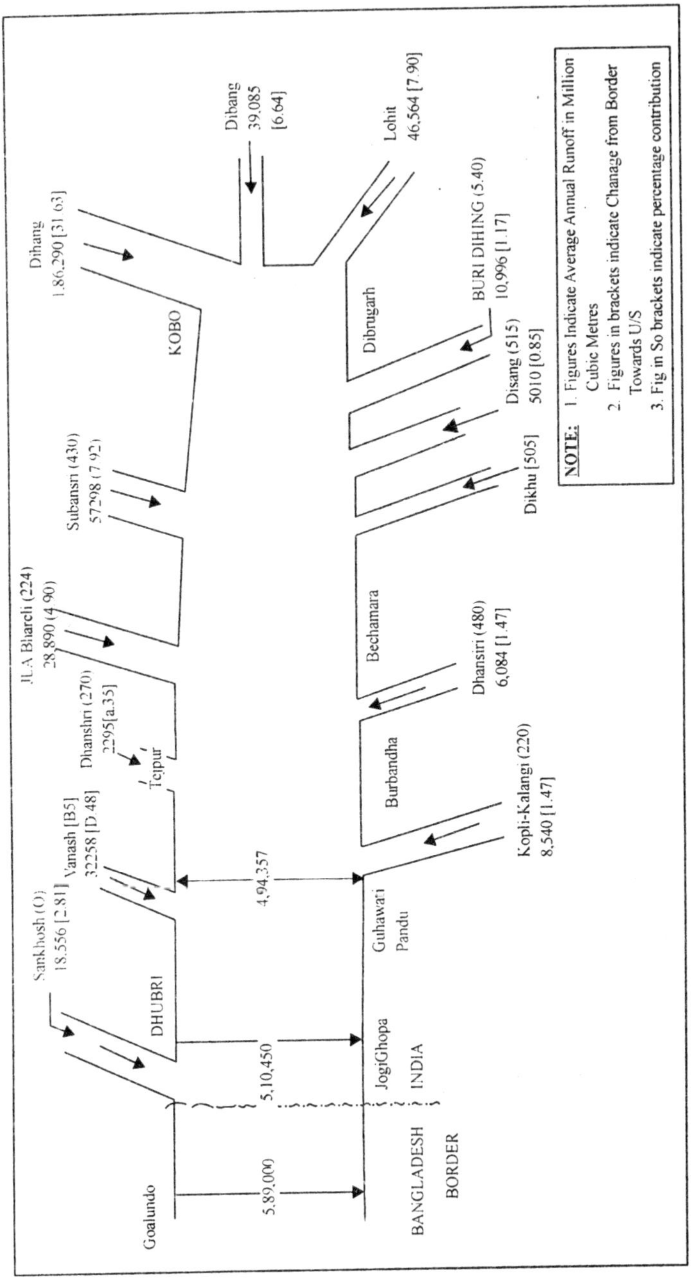

Fig. 2.2 : Average Annual Runoff of Brahmaputra

Karimganj. The Mokru, the Irang, the Tuivai, the Tuirial, the Jiri, the Rukni Sonai, the Katakhal, the Ghagra, the Dhaleswari, the Longai, the Chiri, the Madhura, and the Jathinga are the major tributaries of the Barak in India. The Surma receives the tributaries flowing south from Meghalaya like the Lubha, the Piyain, the Jadukada etc. and Kushiyara receives the flow of the Singla, the Manu, the Dhalai, the Khowai etc. The Surma and the Kushiyara joins under the name Kalni, which receives flows from the Someswari, the Kangsa, the Beluai and the Mogra before assuming the name Meghna. The average annual flow in the Meghna is measured as 3 to 4 M ham at Badarpur in Karimganj District in Assam and is reported as 14.3 M ham at Bhairab Bazar in Bangladesh. The flow is the least during January-February and rises significantly during May-June thereby lending similarity of flow pattern to that of the Brahmaputra.

The combined flow of the Ganga-Brahmaputra joins the Meghna at Chandpur and it continues to flow for another 130 km as one mighty river Meghna before finally debouching into the Bay of Bengal.

Amongst the minor river basins, the Manipur river originates in the hills of Manipur and flows south through the Imphal valley to enter Myanmar near Memdi New. In Myanmar, the river joins the Chindwin which subsequently merges with the Irrawady river to reach the Bay of Bengal.

Land Resources of the North Eastern Region

The North Eastern Region is one of the five electrical regions in the power system of the country constituting the seven states of Arunachal Pradesh, Assam, Manipur, Meghalaya, Mizoram, Nagaland and Tripura. Although Sikkim has recently been brought under the jurisdiction of the North Eastern Council, the state of Sikkim, being in the eastern electric region, has not been included under the purview of this paper. While Arunachal Pradesh, Assam and Meghalaya lie wholly in Brahmaputra-Meghna sub basin, only portion of Manipur, Nagaland, Mizoram and Tripura lie in it. The

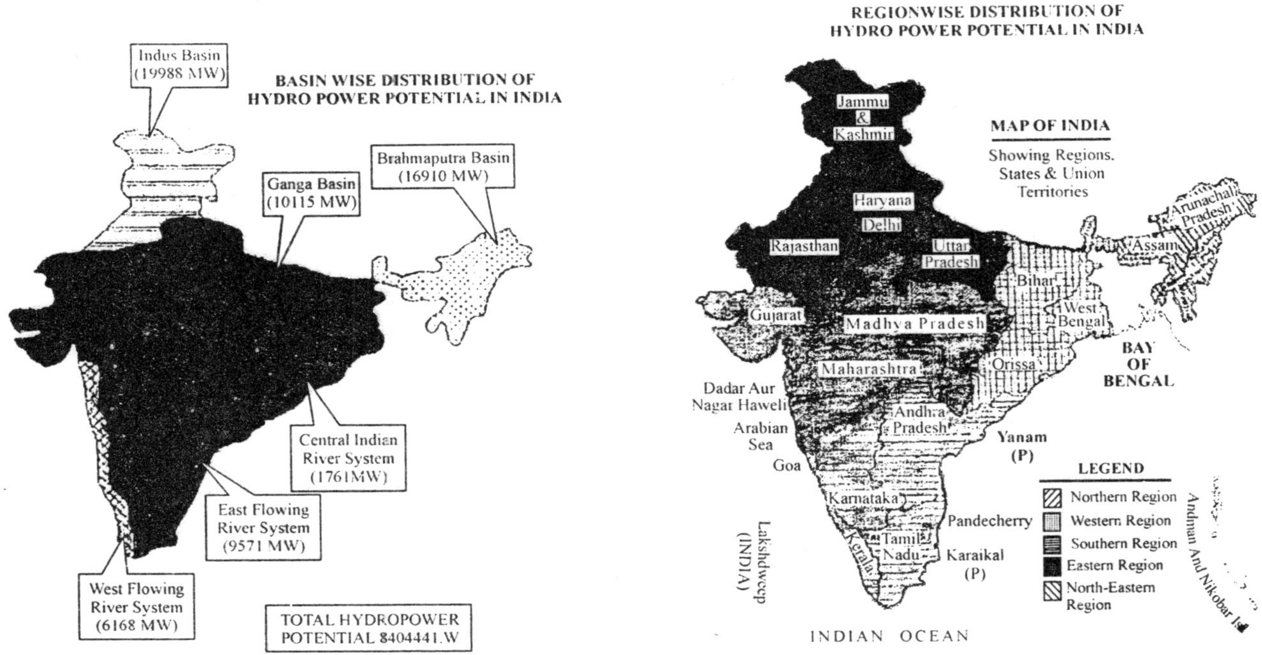

Fig. 2.3 : Basinwise and Regionwise Distribution of Hydro Power Potential in India

geographical areas of these states are given in Table 2.1, which also shows the corresponding population densities based on 1991 census. From the table, it may be observed that the North Eastern Region accounts for only 7.76 per cent of the total geographical area of the counry. Population density is the maximum in Assam, which is more than the national average, followed by Tripura. Arunachal Pradesh has the lowest population density which is about 1/27th from that of the country, the next higher being Mizoram.

Table 2.1 : Geographical Area and Population Density of States of N.E. Region

State	*Area (sq. km.)*	*Population Density (Based on 1991 Census) Persons/sq. km.*
Arunachal Pradesh	83,743	10
Assam	78,438	286
Manipur	22,327	82
Meghalaya	22,429	79
Mizoram	21,081	33
Nagaland	16,579	73
Tripura	10,486	263
Region Total	**255,083**	**123**
All India Total	**3,287,263**	**273**

Geology of the North Eastern Region

Geology study of the rock formations of the North Eastern Region reveals the availability of rocks of different eras ranging from the oldest azoic to the relatively recent caiozoic group. Table 2.2 showing the stratigraphical scale is presented for a quick glance at the age of the rock formations of different systems in different areas.

Part of Meghalaya and Assam falls in Archean system. This consists of the oldest rock formations. Gneiss is most common rock in this system with a great variation in texture and mineral composition. The next common rock of this system is Schist, occurring in a numebr of varieties, e.g., Hornblende Schist, Mica Schist, Chlorite Schist, Talc Schist etc.

Table 2.2 : Geological Time Scale

Group/Era	*System/Period*	*Time Interval From Present (in Years)*
Quarternary	Recent	1,000,000
	Pleistocene	
	Pliocene	
Teritary of Cainozoic	Miocene	35,000,000
	Oligocene	50,000,000
	Eocene	70,000,000
	Creataceous	120,000,000
Secondary or Mesozoic	Jurassic	150,000,000
	Triassic	190,000,000
	Permian	220,000,000
	Carboniferous	280,000,000
Primary or Palaeozoic	Devonian	320,000,000
	Silurian	350,000,000
	Ordovician	400,000,000
	Cambrian	500,000,000
Proterozoic	Pre-Cambrian	1500,000,000
Azoic	Archean	4500,000,000

Rocks of Cambrian system, which are of marine sedimentary origin, are found in parts of Assam and Arunachal Pradesh. This includes Shales, Sandstone, Limestone and Quartzites.

Some regions of Assam are characterised by the rocks of the Permian system. These rocks are of sedimentary origin, containing products of volcanic activity. The rock types include Shales, Limestone, Sandstones, Slates, Quartzites and Basalts.

Stretches of Arunachal Pradesh falls under Triassic system (Tertiary) which includes chiefly Limestone, others being Shales and Sandstone.

Cretaceous system of formation covers a part of Assam where the marine geosynclinal facies includes Shales, Limestones, Conglomerate etc.

Gondwana formation is found in Assam and Arunachal Pradesh which includes mainly shales, sandstone with thick seams of coal.

Major parts of Nagaland, Manipur, Mizoram, Tripura and a part of Assam and Meghalaya are in Eocene system of formation, which displays rocks of both marine and fresh water sedimentary origins. The chief rock types in this sytem are shales, sandstones and limestones. Occasionally these are associated with coal seams. Occurrence of laterite deposit is also frequent.

In this region the Eocene rocks are well developed and are known as the *Jaintia Series* and the *Disang Series*. The former contains shales, limestones, sandstones and thick coal seams while the later is characterised by the presence of a large quantity of shales, sandstones and some slates, mostly unfossiliferous.

The sandstone formation of Ligocene system and shales, sandstones, conglomerates and limestones of the Miocene system are visible in some parts of Assam.

Rocks of Siwalik system are extensively developed all along the foot hills of the Himalayas which are of fluvial origin and includes shales, sandstones and conglomerates.

The rock formation of the North Eastern Region is highly tectonised, mainly due to the forces operating within the earth crust, such as lateral compression, vertical movements, igneous intrusions and salt domes. Several boundary thrusts pass through this region. These consequence to major folds, faults and drags. Thus the rocks of this region cause bulging, caving, etc. on release of the strain these are subjected to. Particularly along the axis of the folds, rocks are highly fractured which makes them weak and allows formation of channel ways for the percolation of surface water. The limestone formations in many locations in the region have solution channels and sink holes.

Hydro Power Potential of the Region

Brahmaptura Basin

The Brahmaputra Basin alone accounts for 34,920 MW of potential hydropower out of the total of 84,044 MW of the entire country as per present assessment at 60 per cent load factor. Exlcuding the sub-basins of the Brahmaputra falling outside the North Eastern Region, the hydropower in the region is assessed at 31,857 MW at 60 per cent load factor. The contribution from small schemes i.e. potential small rivers/streams, canal falls, pumped storage schemes etc. is however not included in the assessed potential as projected for the region. The enormity of this hydropower potential in the north eastern region is depicted in the basin wise and region wise distribution shown diagrammatically in Fig. 2.3. Stating in terms of the political sub-division of the region, Arunachal Pradesh tops the list in terms of hydro-power potential with 26,757 MW followed by Mizoram, while Tripura possesses the least potential amount to 9 MW, all assessed at 60 per cent load factor. Fig. 2.4 shows the statewise break-up of the hydro power potential of the region.

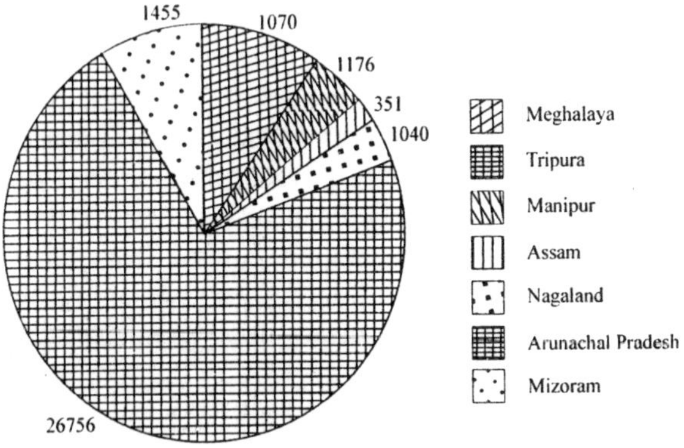

Fig. 2.4 : Statewise Hydro Potential of the Region

In attempting to present a brief account of the major hydro power potential of the region, we start at a downstream reach of the Brahmaputra and move upstream along the south-bank pointing at the potential sites for development of hydro power. The Umium-Umtru-Khri valley located in Meghalaya has a potential of 400 MW installed capacity out of which 174 MW is already developed in cascading stages. This is exclusive of the 11.2 MW isolated development in Umtru Power Station. The Kapili valley has a potential of 458 MW, a significant portion of which is already developed and a portion of the balance is presently under development. The Borapani river, also known as the Langpi, a tributary which joins the Kolong before its confluence with the Brahmaputra has possibility of developing three hydro power projects. The upper and the intermediate stages of the Borapani valley will yield 120 MW in 2 power stations and the 3rd, called he Barbi - Langpi Project can have an installed capacity of 100 MW.

A 120 MW hydro project can be located at the confluence of the Umswai river with the Umium, known as the Killing at the lower reaches.

On the south-bank of the Brahmapura, the next potential site is the Doyang Hydro Project with 75 MW installed capacity in Wokha district in Nagaland, which is nearing completion.

Travelling upstream along the Brahmaputra, the Noa Dihin river has a potential of 100 MW, if a 152 metre high dam is constructed near Miao in Arunachal Pradesh.

Further upstream, the Lohit, known as the Tellu in the higher reaches has a potential of 520 MW as proposed by the name Demwe Hydro Project by the NEEPCO, if a 34.0 metre high gated weir is constructed at a site 67.5 km from Tezu. The Brahmapura Board has, however, planned for a multipurpose dam on the Lohit with a power station having an installed capacity of 3000 MW.

Travelling upstream along the north-bank from West to East, the first tributary with a major hydro power project is the Manas. With a 266 m high dam at Mathanguri at the Indo-Bhutan border, a power station of 5000 MW installed capacity can be made. In the Jia-Bhareli or the Kameng basin, a 600 MW hydro power project is soon to be taken up for development with two dams, one on the Enga and other on the Bichom tributary of the Kameng. In the lower reaches a 211 m high dam is possible on the Jia-Bhareli river for making a power station with 2000 MW installed capacity.

The Ranganadi, a tributary of the Brahmaputra in Arunachal Pradesh, has a cascade development scheme with a potential of 405 MW installation. The Stage-I of the scheme is a run of the river scheme and is nearing completion with a 68 m high dam of 41 km on the Kimin-Ziro road and power house at Hoz on the bank of the Dikrong river. This proejct thus involves inter-basin transfer. In Stage-II, the Ranganadi will have a 180 MW project with a 134 m high dam across the river at Yazali.

The Dikrong tributary in the adjacent valley has a potential of 100 MW if a 48.5 m high dam is constructed across the river near Yayee village in Arunachal Pradesh.

A 240 m high dam at 3 km upstream of Gerukamuk on the Subansiri river, if constructed, will facilitate installation of a 4800 MW power station on the right bank of the Subansiri.

The Dibang Project has potential of 2500 MW with the construction of a storage dam 231 m high about 3 km upstream of Kronli in Arunachal Pradesh.

The Siang or the Dihand offers prospect for one of the largest hydro power schemes in the world providing for an installation of 20,000 MW power station with the construction of a 262 m high storage dam about 50 km upstream of Passighat in Arunachal Pradesh.

The installation capacities of the major projects identified in the Brahmaputra Basin are enlisted in Table 2.3.

Table 2.3 : Sources of Major Hydro Power Potential on the Brahmaputra

North Bank			*South Bank*		
Tributary	*Installed Capacity (MW)*	*State*	*Tributary*	*Installed Capacity (MW)*	*State*
Dihang	20,000	Arunachal Pradesh	Lohit	3,000	Arunachal Pradesh
Manas	5,000	Arunachal Pradesh	Damwe[$]	520	Arunachal Pradesh
Subansiri	4,800	Arunachal Pradesh	Kopili[@]	485	Assam
Talin	3,500	Arunachal Pradesh	Umiam-Umtru-Khri[@]	400	Meghalaya
Rikor	2,700	Arunachal Pradesh	Langpi[+]	220	Assam
Dibang	2,500	Arunachal Pradesh	Killing	120	Assam
Jia-Bhareli	2,000	Arunachal Pradesh	Noa-Dihing	100	Arunachal Pradesh
Idipo	1,150	Arunachal Pradesh	Doyang[+]	75	Nagaland
Kameng[#]	600	Arunachal Pradesh			
Ranganadi[']	585	Arunachal Pradesh			
Upper Subbasiri	500	Arunachal Pradesh			
Pakke	105	Arunachal Pradesh			
Dikrong[$]	100	Arunachal Pradesh			
Papumpam[$]	100	Arunachal Pradesh			

Legend

@ Generating Project
\# Projects under Execution
\+ Execution being taken up soon
$ D.P.R. under Finalisation

Barak Basin

In the Barak basin, a power proejct with 1500 MW installation capacity can be developed by constructing a 158 m high storage dam near Tipaimukh in Assam.

Tuivai project on the river Tuivai in Mizoram will have a 155 m high dam near Ngopa village for generation of 210 MW of hydro power. The Tuirial Project on the river Tuirial in Mizoram is being taken up for development which will have a 77 m high dam and a power house with 60 MW installed capacity. The Dhaleswari river project, also in Mizoram, has a proposed installation capacity of 80 MW.

The Loktak hydro electric project in Manipur with 105 MW installed capacity is already commissioned. The Loktak downstream project with propose installation of a 100 MW generating capacity will divert the flow to the Barak River and is therefore included under the projects in the Barak basin.

The Kynshai project with 600 MW installed capacity and the Leska project with 75 MW installed capacity are important sources of hydro power potential in the Barak basin located in Meghalaya and proposed for development.

Table 2.4 : Sources of Major Hydro Power Potential on the Barak

Tributary	Installed Capacity (MW)	State
Tipaimukh#	1,500	Trijunction of Assam, Manipur and Mizoram
Kynshai	600	Meghalaya
Tuivai#	210	Mizoram
Dhaleswari	150	Mizoram
Loktak@	100	Manipur
Loktak downstream#		Manipur
Irang	100	Manipur
Leska#	75	Meghalaya
Tuirial+	60	Mizoram

Legend

@ Generating Projects.

+ Projects under Execution.

Execution being taken up soon.

In Manipur, the Irang river in the Barak basin offers possibility of a 100 MW hdyro power project. The major sources of hydro power potential in the Barak basin are enlisted in Table 2.4.

Status of Hydro Power Scenario in the North Eastern Region

The total installed capacity of the hydro power stations as on 30th April 1998 are shown in Table 2.5.

Table 2.5 : Installed Hydro Capacity of the NE Region (As on 30th April, 1998)

Sl. No.	*Constituents*	*On Grid (MW)*	*Isolated (MW)*	*Constituent Total (MW)*
1.	Arunachal Pradesh	—	23.55	23.55
2.	Assam	—	2.00	2.00
3.	Manipur	—	2.80	2.80
4.	Meghalaya	185.2	1.51	186.71
5.	Mizoram	—	5.38	5.38
6.	Nagaland	—	3.30	3.30
7.	Tripura	15.0	1.00	15.00
8.	NEEPCO	250.00	—	250.00
9.	NHPC	105.0	—	105.00
North Eastern Regional Total (MW)		555.20	38.03	593.23

Source : System Status Report of N.E. Region by the P.G.C.I. Ltd.

The break-up of the relatively significant grid contributions of the constituents are shown in Fig. 2.5.

Besides the aforesaid total of 593.23 MW already developed, executions of a few other projects are on, the details of which are given in Table 2.6.

The break-up of the installed capacity in the North-Eastern Region as on 31st March, 1997, and the share of hydro sector is shown in Fig. 2.6.

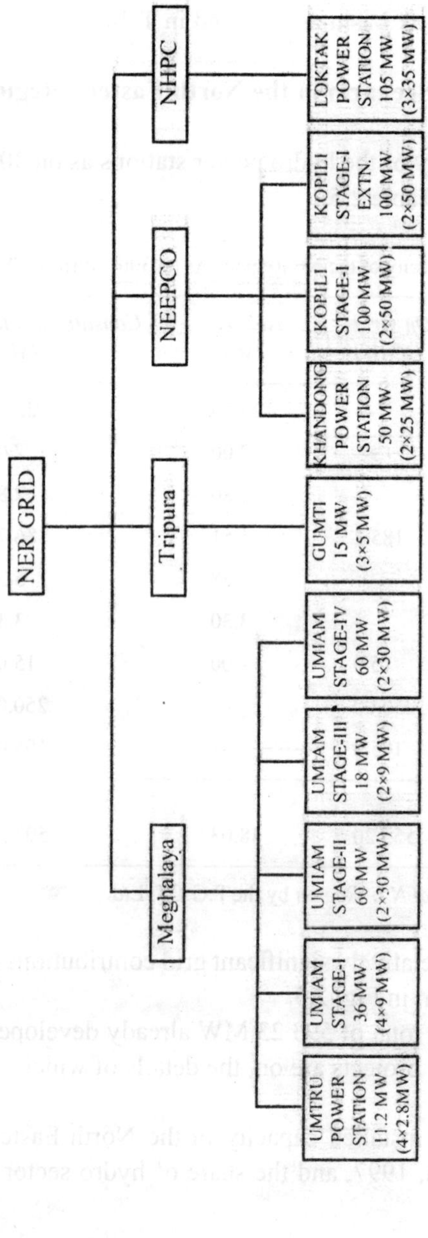

Fig. 2.5 : Grid Contribution of the Constituents in NE Region

Table 2.6 : Ongoing Projects

Project	*State*	*Installed Capacity (MW)*
Ranganadi Stage-II	Arunachal Pradesh	405 MW
Doyang	Nagaland	75 MW
Karbi Langpi	Assam	100 MW
Dhansiri	Assam	19.95 MW
Tuirial	Mizoram	60 MW
Nuranang Hydel	Arunachal Pradesh	6 MW
Dalaima Micro Hydel	Assam	0.60 MW

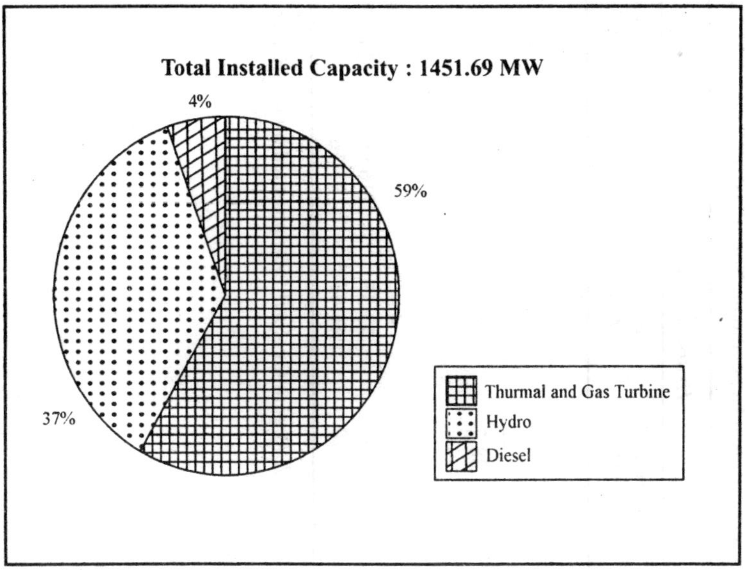

Fig. 2.6 : Break-up of Installed Capacity in North-East Region (As on 31.3.1997)

Performance of the Hydro Projects in the North-Eastern Region

The overall performance of the generating hydro power projects is satisfactory. A sample comparison of the performances of the hydro projects vis-a-vis the thermal projects in the region, contribution to the grid for the month of April 1998 is given in Table 2.7.

Table 2.7 : The Scheduled *versus* Actual Generationin North-Eastern Region, April, 1998

Constituents	*Hydro Generation*			*Thermal Generation*		
	Scheduled (MU)	*Actual (MU)*	*Per cent Achieved*	*Scheduled (MU)*	*Actual (MU)*	*Per cent Achieved*
Arunachal Pradesh	—	—	—	—	—	—
Assam	—	—	—	108.9	97.5	89.53
Manipur	—	—	—	—	—	—
Meghalaya	38.7	39.65	102.45	—	—	—
Mizoram	—	—	—	—	—	—
Nagaland	—	—	—	—	—	—
Tripura	5.00	4.46	89.20	21.70	18.55	85.48
NEEPCO	33.90	73.55	216.96	116.70	48.42	41.49
NHPC	47.70	44.44	93.16	—	—	—

Source : System Status Report of NE Region for April 1998 prepared by the PGCI Ltd.

Growing Need of Power on the North-Eastern Region

The total energy consumptions in the month of April for the last three consecutive years are shown in Fig. 2.7 which reflects the growing trend.

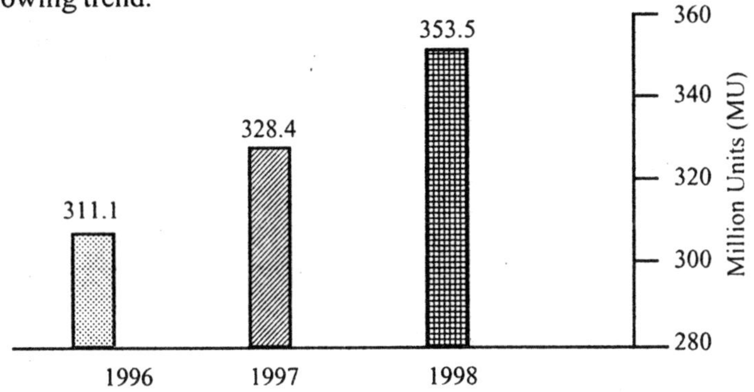

Fig. 2.7 : Trend of Energy Consumption in the NE Region

The projection of the energy requirement in MU and the peak load in MW towards public utilities during the ends of the ongoing 9th and the two forthcoming Five Year Plan periods for the states in the North Eastern Region are presented in Table 2.8. The projects of the energy requirement in MU for the different regions for the country and the country as a whole are shown in Fig. 2.8 and the corresponding values of the peak demand in MW are shown in Fig. 2.9.

Table 2.8 : Projections of the Energy and Peak Load Requirement in North-Eastern Region

State	*Energy Requirement (MU)*			*Peak Load (MW)*		
	2001-02 End of 9th Plan	*2006-07 End of 10th Plan*	*2011-12 End of 11th Plan*	*2001-02 End of 9th Plan*	*2006-07 End of 10th Plan*	*2011-12 End of 11th Plan*
Arunachal Pradesh	346	596	982	94	151	249
Assam	4976	6818	9124	986	1330	1765
Manipur	703	1201	2024	193	323	531
Meghalaya	638	912	1279	140	196	270
Mizoram	505	1016	1872	141	267	465
Nagaland	268	372	507	68	93	126
Tripura	712	1147	1765	186	292	438
Region	**8148**	**12062**	**17553**	**1722**	**2527**	**3661**

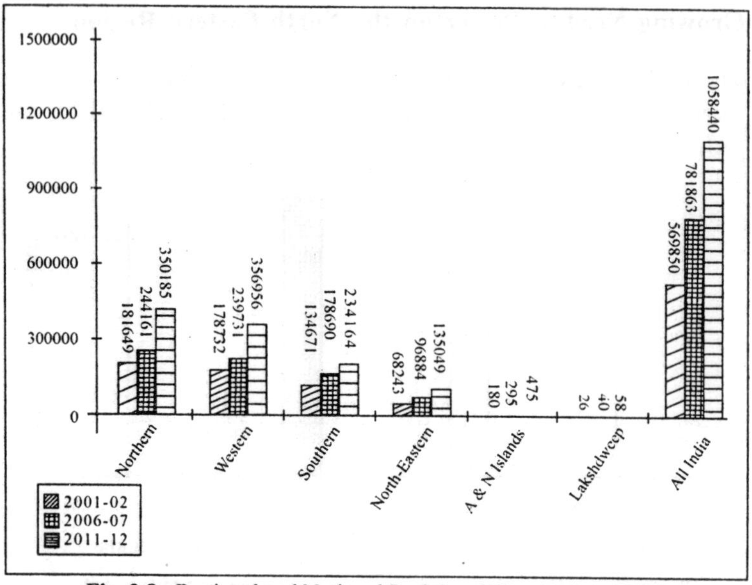

Fig. 2.8 : Regional and National Peak Load Requirement (MU)

Source : Fifteenth Electric Power Survey of India by the CEA.

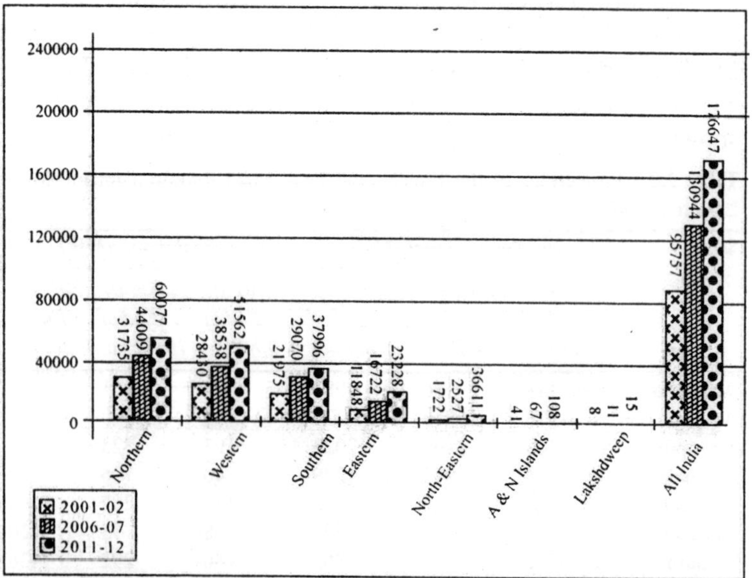

Fig. 2.9 : Regional and National Peak Load Requirement (MW)

The energy available for the year 1996-97 was 4189.61 MU as against the requirement of 4666.44 MU for the year. The energy requirements for the region in 2001-02 is proejcted as 8148 MU, which is expected to rise steadily to 12062 MU in 2006-07 and 17553 MU in 2011-12 as reflected in Fig. 2.8.

Similarly the peak demand met for the year 1996-97 was 776 MW (October, 1996) as against the peak demand of 840 MW (October, 1996) for the year. The peak demand for the region in 2001-02 is proejcted as 1722 MW, which is expected to increase to 2527 MW in 2006-07 and 3661 MW in 2011-12 as presented in Fig. 2.9.

The growth of the power sector in the North-Eastern Region over the years is by far steady. This is reflected in Fig. 2.10 However, as reflected in Fig. 2.6 the share of the hydro sector in the overall power scenario is still loomy and this is veritably so when viewed in the prespective of the enormous hydro potential in the region.

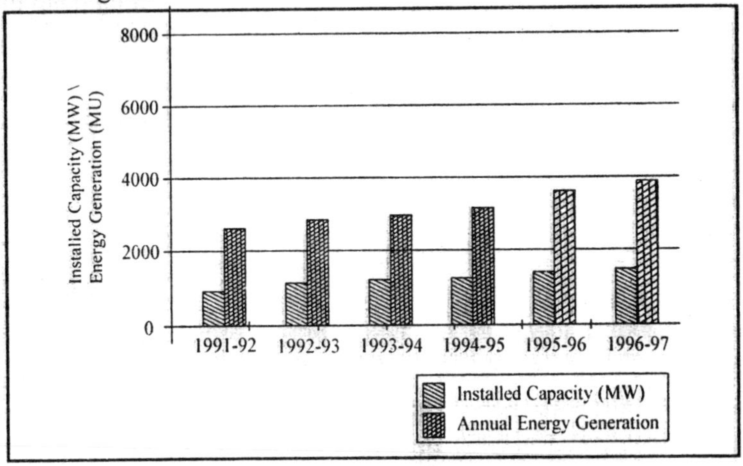

Fig. 2.10 : Growth of Installed Capacity and Energy Generation in North-Eastern Region

In response to the demand in excess of the supply of electric power by the region for the region, huge import of energy needs to be resorted to from the Eastern grid to the North Eastern grid. This may be seen from the representative values taken for the year

1996-97, furnished in Table 2.9.

Table 2.9 : Projections of the Energy and Peak Load requirement in North-Eastern Region

Month	*Import from Eastern Grid*	*Export to the Eastern Grid*	*Net Import from Eastern Region*
Apr. 96	17.44	5.67	11.77
May 96	10.95	8.19	2.76
June 96	21.10	1.36	19.74
July 96	31.88	1.72	30.16
Aug. 96	33.88	2.07	631.81
Sept. 96	20.41	3.24	17.17
Oct. 96	36.27	1.97	34.30
Nov. 96	30.03	1.74	28.29
Dec. 96	55.56	0.15	55.41
Jan. 97	51.08	0.44	50.64
Feb. 97	41.15	0.69	40.46
Mar. 97	40.24	0.85	39.39
Total	**389.99**	**28.09**	**361.90**

Source : Annual Report of NEREB for the year 1996-97.

The regional power scenario in the North Eastern Region thus calls for rapid increase in the installation capacities of the power projects with special emphasis on the hydro power sector.

In the national perspective, the staggering high demand of peak load estimated at 95,757 MW during 2001-02, 1,30,944 MW during 2006-07 and 1,76,647 MW during 2011-12 need immediate attention in planning and investment decision-making in power from so as to narrow the gap between demand and the supply. In terms of thermal-hydro mix, the present ratio is about 75:25 as against an ideal ratio of 60:40.

Due to various constraints generation of power through the thermal power stations owned by the states in the North Eastern Region, there is a constant shortfall of 75 to 150 MW of power during peak load. An analysis by the CEA of the peak availability and the peak demand in the region indicates that the region will have surplus power during 1999-2000 and 2000-2001, after all the ongoing projects are commissioned. However, there will be a continuous deficit thereafter, reaching 22 per cent of peak load deficit and 17 per cent energy deficit by 2006-07.

In order to improve the long-term power scenario of the region, in order to contribute to the national grid to mitigate the energy demand and peak load requirement of the country and to take corrective measures for a balanced thermal-hydro mix for optimum power generation, subsequent to the grid connection of the North Eastern Region with the best of the mainland, development of the enormous hydro power potential of the North Eastern Region is of utmost necessity.

Why Hydro Power

- Hydro power is stated to be a green power as it is obtained from non-polluting resource with high conversion efficiency. It does not contribute to the Green House effect.
- Hydro power is environment friendly, if planned and executed systematically.
- The total potential in the country is enormous with about 420 billion units of annual generation potential which is about 1.5 times the present use of the electricity in the country.
- It is produced from a perennial source and the hydro power generation is perpetual. When fully developed, hydro power can save 250 million tonnes equivalent of oil consumed annually for thermal power generation. Coal reserves in India are only 1.5 per cent of the world's total reserves against the population share of 16-17 per cent and needs conservation.
- Hydro power development, in most cases, is an integral and important part of multipurpose water resource projects. With storage facilities in large projects, flood waves may be retained for moderation of severe floods in the region. Irrigation, river regulation, navigation, pisciculture, wildlife preservation, recreational facilities, municipal water use etc. can be augmented by the storage in the impounding reservoirs and pondages created for hydro power development.
- Hydro power plants normally have long life of equipments.

With the dam, tunnels, underground caverns and concrete works having useful life spans of a century or more needing very little maintenance, hydro power projects usually have long life.

- The cost of generation of hydro energy is relatively low and so is the cost of operation and maintenance of hydro stations.
- The cost hydro energy is fairly stable and is free from inflationary pressure of economy.
- Apart from conservation of perishable resources, large scale development of hydro power would provide substantial relief to the transport sector and reduce the hassels of mine development as well.
- Hydro power technology is well developed and proven with overall efficiency of about 90 per cent compared to about 30 per cent of thermal stations, 30-34 per cent for gas turbines and 42-44 per cent for combined cycle plants.
- MDC (Minimum Daily Consumption) condition in respect of accepting the supply of natural gas for gas based power projects may require the thermal stations to generate at levels which may not be economically viable and may not be optimum in terms of system contribution. The thermal power stations cannot be run economically below a certain minimum load factor. A predominant hydro system is hence superior to a predominant thermal station.
- Hydro power stations can quickly respond to the changing loads and hence are ideally suited for peaking. A healthy mix of thermal and hydro generation by affecting substantial increase in the present level of hydro power generation is highly desirable for enhancing the system reliability. The declining trend of percentage of hydro power share, therefore, needs to be arrested and reversed in the forthcoming plan periods.
- Hydro power projects in the North Eastern Region will invariably be located in remote, far flung, difficult and inaccessible areas. Development of hydro projects will greatly improve the infrastructure and the communication facilities in the region and give much needed boost to the socio-economic scenario.
- Hydro power projects are labour intensive and provide employment opportunity.

- In the O&M stage, the operation of the hydro power stations is much simpler requiring a small operating man power.
- From national perspective, the limitations of regional planning in the power front as briefed below may be got over by developing hydro power potential and the associated grid network throughout the country.
  — Although regions have shortage of peak loads, yet, at the same time some of the regions back down their generation during off peak hours.
  — A relatively higher amount of installed capacity is required to meet the peak load in the regional grids.
  — Thermal machines are strained due to large variations in load corresponding to peaking an off peak periods.
  — Uneconomic generation leads to higher costs.

The development of hydro power potential of the rivers in the north east is therefore the need of the hour for all round development of the region in particular and the country in general.

A comparison of various sources of energy in India is given in Table 2.10.

Prejudices against Hydro Development and their Weaknesses

Planners, decision makers and power engineers are not to be carried away by the euphoria of every aspect of hydro development being beneficial, economic and bright, lest they should be accused of being unfairly biased. Due attention needs to be paid to the prejudices against hydro power development and measures need to be contemplated and schemes need to be conceived to minimise the damages which may have the possibilities to be associated with such development.

- Hydro power stations are stated to be at the disposal of the vagaries of weather. Although the fact is true, the same holds good for thermal stations as well, which manifest in the problems of wet coal and choking of bunkers in monsoon.
- The gestation period of hydro-electric project is stated to be

long and associated with blockade of funds for longer period as well as delay in deriving benefits from the projects.

Table 2.10 : Comparison of Various Sources of Energy

Energy Sources	*Life in years*	*Magnitude*	*Major Advantages and Disadvantages in brief*
Coal / Thermal	150 Years	Limited to about 60 per cent of power generation	It cannot be used for peaking power, higher emission of CO_2, SO_2 and dust. It contributes to 40 per cent of pollution, O&M is costly. It operates at lower capacity.
Nuclear	100 Years	20,000 MW	It generates half the installed capacity, number of safe guards. It causes safety hazards and acid rains. There is a waste disposal problem from raidiation point of view.
Non-Conventional Energy			
Mini-hydro	Renewable	5000 MW	It is used in a remote area locally. But not popular.
Wind Energy	Renewable	20,000 MW	Utility is only 16 to 20 per cent. It is not connected to grid. It is utilised locally.
Solar Energy	Renewable	5000 kWHr/Yr	It is very costly. Cost ranging from Rs. 20 crores to Rs. 25 crore per MW. It is not viable commercially.
Hydro Power	Renewable	84,000 MW	It is environment friendly and cheaper. It can be used for peaking power. Maintenance is very cheap.

Source : "Implements in development of hydro power — The green power and their remedies" by Sri Yogendra Prasad and Dr. P. N. Darde in *"Proceedings of the Conference on Hydro Power Development (24-25 April, 1997)"* organised by CBIP.

A point in countering this allegation is that, a considerable length of time is spent in creating proper infratructure for taking up main works of a hydro-electric scheme, most of which are located in inaccessible and difficult terrains which is very much true for the North Eastern Region. However, developments of infrastructure invariably improves the quality of life of the people in and around such locations and thus fulfils the social objectives considerably. Hence the time required for development of infrastructure should not, in true sense, be included in defining the gestation period of a project and the "zero" date for execution should start from the date the works for the major civil structures is taken up. The gestation period for a hydro power scheme with such a rational and positive approach will then not be projected as long and will be comparable to those for thermal and nuclear power schemes.

- Hydro projects are stated to be highly capital intensive requiring huge initial investments.
  This is belied by the fact that per kW cost reduces with the increase in size of units for the power stations. A study conducted by the Council of Power Utility on Cost/kW of generation indicated that hydro projects in medium capacity range (50-100 MW) are cheaper than their thermal counterparts.

The thermal power schemes need development of new mines, deplete the perishable resources of coal and gas, burden the transport sector and contribute to the green house effect considerably. In view of the above, in taking into account the auxilirary factors and infrastructural developments in either case, and in realisation of multifarious benefits accrued from hydro projects, the hydro sector calls for greater attetnion for development.

Hindrances to the Hydro Development in the N.E. Region

The major hindrances to the development of hydro power in the North Eastern Region are highlighted in the following paragraphs:

Adverse Geological Conditions

The presence of a number of different rock formations of different systems which are not very suitable for carrying out complex construction activities and locating major civil structures, which are pre-requisites for development of hydro power schemes, pose major challenges before the engineers and the project managers during execution of the works. Although every care is taken in adequately logging the areas to be taken up for construction activities, yet unpredictable, precarious and treacherous formations, more often than not, appear during execution in real life situations as experienced with the power projects which are either developed or are under development in the north eastern region.

The formations of Chlorite schist, Talc schist etc., when contacted with percolating surface water or ground water flow, become very soft and fragile while the mica schists, mostly being very thinly foliated, result in book page type of failure and thus pose serious problems in tunnelling works in particular and excavation works of other structures in general.

The Gondwana formation is the rock type most despised by the tunnelling engineers. Unfortunately such formations are encountered in the hills of the region which retard the development activities to a great extent. Explosions of methane gas in the Gondwana zone has also been experienced during works of tunnelling in the Ranganandi H.E. project and special cares with special equipments needed to be taken to safely carry out the boring works. Besides tackling the problem in some of the stretches, the alignment of the head race tunnel itself in the Ranganadi H.E. project needed to be changed significantly to avoid the Gondwana formation in other stretches.

The problem of solubility of limestone formations, resulting in creation of solution channel and sink holes, is the other important factor which hinders the prospect of hydro power development in the region. The competency of two reservoirs of the Kopili H.E. project in Assam needed to be established after very detailed time and fund consuming investigations to ascertain that there would be no leakage from the reservoirs because of this kind of problem, before the project could be taken up. At stages, serious doubts were even raised, as to whether the project would at all be implemented at the end. Costly reservoir treatments were also resorted to in order to avert any possible damage because of creation of solution channels and sink holes in the reservoir areas. This problem of presence of soluble limestone formations also restricts the selection of locations for dams and hence the reservoirs in otherwise very attractive sites on the river course for planning hydro power projects in the region.

Presence of huge overburdens and alluvial deposits over foundation grade rocks in river beds becomes a major factor in deciding the location and the type of dam in many major rivers in the region identified as sources of huge hydro power potential. The associated involvement of high costs in such cases is also a deterring factor.

Under circumstances, some of which are briefed above, on site decisions as also the major decisions in managerial level assume vital importance in risk sharing and in keeping intact the viability of the project as anticipated in the planning stage. Judicious selection of sites by experienced professionals, coupled with adoption of new technologies and methodologies, however can well combat this drawback from adverse geological conditions point of view.

Difficult Terrains

Hydro electric projects are generally located in remote inaccessible places. The terrain of the North Eastern Region, having prospects of development of hydro electric power, is no exception. Several difficulties caused by such inaccessibility are faced during pre-construction as well as construction stages, in carrying huge quantities of construction materials and equipments. The remoteness of the sites fails to provide the minimum basic necessities for the personnels engaged for development of projects and affects the efficiency if not properly attended to. However, this cannot be attributed as a major hindrance by proper infrastructure development planning. Instances of such bottleneck being overcome may be found elsewhere as in Sawalkot in J&K where a power project of

600 MW required construction of 126 km of road along with 17 numbers of bridges and in Dhauli Ganga Stage-I H.E. project in Uttar Pradesh, which required construction of 292 km of road and 65 numbers of bridges, for development of a 280 MW power project.

Investigation

Success of a hydro power project depends largely on the efficacy and accuracy during investigations of the hydrometeorology, geology, construction materials etc., based on which the status and the structure of the project is designed. Unfortunately, due emphasis is not being given to the investigation phase for development of hydro projects in the North Eastern Region in particular and the country as a whole. Such lackadaisical attitudes result in improper investigations leading to major changes in structural features of the projects, methodologies and techniques during construction phases and consequent time and cost overruns. However, provision of adequate facilities to the investigating personnel for efficient discharging of duties assigned, introduction of state-of-the-art equipment for accurate measurements and proper supervision at various levels will extract the best outputs from the field staff.

Seismic Aspects

Most of the parts of the North Eastern Region are earthquake prone and falls in Zone of the Seismological map of India. The older rocks in the foothills of the Himalayas are thrusted against the younger rocks of the Siwalik system accusing the long thrust fault know as the "Great Boundary Fault". The surroundings of this zone is highly seismic. However, aseismic design methodologies, which are being incorporated during design stage of the hydro projects in the North Eastern Region, are meant for reducing the seismic impacts and hence this aspect may not be construed as a serious drawback.

Land Availability

The tribal land holding system, prevalent in parts of the North Eastern region, poses difficulties in acquiring land for development of projects in the region. The Doyang Project in Nagaland is one such, in which delay in land acquisition caused the project to be delayed by about two years. The non-availability of non-forest land to be utilised for afforestation and problems in rehabilitating the Project Affected People (PAP) in locations suitable and acceptable to them also causes difficulties in commencing the project.

Low Power Demand

The industrial growth in the North Eastern Region has not been significant as compared to many other parts of the country. The demand of power is consequently low in comparison. However, development of cnormous potential of hydro power in the region should not be stalled with this plea as such developments are sure to improve the socio-economic life of the people of the region and attract investments in industrial sector with resultant growth which are highly desirable. Such developments will also allow export of hydro power to the other parts of the country through the natinoal grid.

Contractural Matters

Physical as well as price contigencies in contractual matters often cause indefinite delay and consequent escalations in cost. Sometimes the method of tender finalisation engages incompetent contractors with inadequate resources in major and/or specialised works. Inadequate mechanisms for sorting out contractual problems and incorrect assessment by the contractors before taking up a job, ambiguity in specifications and clauses of contract agreement etc. become major concern and cause for unwarranted delays. Finalisation of contracts by experienced professionals in respective fields in the light of recent developments avert the possibilities of confusions, litigations and consequent time and cost overruns.

Construction Planning and Techniques

Very often, a very unrealistic construction programme is adopted for hydro power schemes in the planning stage in order to project them as viable and attractive which prove to be far deviated from the actual during construction stages. Choice of matching construction equipments and involvement of contractors should be part of construction planning. On the excuse of availability of cheap man power in the country, the development of hydro sector has suffered setback during the last four decades in matters related to construction technologies because of utilisation of obsolete, misfitting and inefficient machineries. Till date the machineries with state-of-the-art technologies, widely used in the developed countries, such as the TBM (Tunnel Boring Machine), are matters of seminar and discourse in our country. In many projects, import of some of these machineries became the privileges of the foreign contractors without any cost control. However, corrective measures may be taken for development of hydro power projects in the North Eastern Region and NEEPCO has taken bold steps to import many such machines without involving any foreign contractor.

Organisational Problems

Improper deployment of man power very often becomes cause of delay and lack of co-ordination. In multipurpose projects, multi-pronged control of execution activities dilutes the responsibilities and hampers the development. On the part of implementing agencies, delay in issuing engineering drawings, inadequate monitoring of construction activities, failure to establish effective and active cost control cell, inefficiency planning of execution works, lack of co-ordination between various wings of the agency, weak and improper managerial decisions, lack of accountability, non-appreciation of creative ideas and feats in achieving important milestones, steps and attitudes likely to hurt the interests of the employees, morbid fear of introducing newer concepts and facilities, frequent transfer of senior and key personnel, absence of a core group of multi-disciplinary nature for planning and resource allocation, reluctance and quiescence in imparting quality training to the personnel etc. are major causes which retard the process of implementation of a project. These are the problems which the implementing agency may effectively attend to for betterment and proper implementation of a scheme.

Environmental Issues

In developing country like India, the environmental guidelines are far more stringent than even the U.S.A. causing delays in finalisation of schemes. In view of diverse conditions in respect of forest cover, population density, level of ecological degradation etc., uniformity of stringency of environmental rules and regulations as applicable to the whole of the country needs to be reviewed. From the perspective of developmental clearance to the hydro power projects by adopting a rational and positive approach is very much desired. The issues related to the environmental aspects such as rehabilitation of the Project Affected People (PAP), submergence, deforestation, raising of downstream flow levels specially in case of inter basin transfers etc. are often being unduly capitalised by vested interests which bring sense of insecurity amongst the local population causing uncertainty to the project implementation. Proper steps need to be taken to educate the masses in right direction, enlighten them regarding the very purpose of the project with the associated benefits and remove apprehensions and misgivings caused by misleading statements and incitements. Environmental Impact Assessment (EIA), Catchment Area Treatment (CAT) Plan, Environmental Management Plan (EMP), Disaster Management Plans (DMP) etc. should also encompass environmental issues adequately.

Law and Order

Extremism plaguing the North Eastern Region repulses participation of power engineers and contractors of national and international reputes for the power development of the region. The Doyang H.E. project in Nagaland suffered immensely because of deteriorated law and order in the locality causing unnecessary delay in commissioning. Efforts from all concerned towards improving the situation is vital for healthy development of the hydro power scenario in the region.

Interstate Disputes

The grant of statehood for the smaller fragments has aggravated the interstate disputes regarding the share of water resources of rivers traversing through them. This has not only crippled some projects but also many attractive projects are on the verge of abandonment before being implemented. Tipaimukh H.E. project located in the tri-junction of the states of Assam, Manipur and Mizoram is one such, implementation of which could not be taken up till date despite prospect of development of 1500 MW of hydro-electric power and other associated benefits. Proper formulation of share of benefits to be derived from such projects acceptable to the concerned states, either at the initiative of the states themselves or at the behest of the central government is necessary in such situations.

Political Interference and Aspirations

Political interference and political pressurization in matters related to awards of major contracts for major works sometimes prove to be stumbling blocks in execution of a project. Such influences should not affect the sanctity of vital decisions towards implementation of hydro power projects.

Aspirations of political activists towards getting a project with lesser gestation period commissioned during tenure for acclaiming the credit for political gain often trashes the issues of development of hydro power in the back-burner and lends support to the implement action of thermal power project with complete disregard to thermal hydro mix, system optimality and other associated unpalatable facts. Much needed thrust at political forums to take up hydro power projects for implementation is therefore found lacking. Political will with distant vision of all round development of the people and political interests are necessary to develop the hydro power sector vital for sustainable development of the region and the country as well.

Funding

With the equity fraction of the debt-equity breakup of the capitalised cost of the project getting lower and lower, adequate arrangements of huge fund required for execution of hydro power projects need to be made through financial institutions both domestic and foreign. Long-term investment decisions, uncertainities and risk sharing inherent in hydro power developments fail to attract prospective investors and thus cause impediments in smooth implementation of hydro power projects. Component of Interest During Construction (IDC) in the overall cost becomes significantly high for such a project. Concerted effort towards reducing the time of completion of hydro power projects and ensuring its viability is therefore very important.

Financial Management

Financial mismanagement, constraints in fund flow and improper resource mobilisation hamper smooth implementation of projects. This aspect needs special attention for success of a hydro power project.

Statutory Clearances

Delay in according statutory clearances by concerned authorities and in acquiring the same by the implementing agencies cause projects to be delayed. Collection and furnishing of adequate and accurate information for Techno Economic Clearance (TEC), Forest and Environmental Clearance, Clearance by the Cabinet Committee on Economic Afairs (CCEA), clearance by the Public Investment Board (PIB), defence clearance for projects in strategically important locations etc., timely scrutiny of the furnished data, quick decisions and recommendations are therefore important in getting a hydro-electric project implemented.

Weather and Nature's Fury

Long monsoon period in the North Eastern Region results in shorter working season which is an impediment in carrying out and co-ordinating the construction activities of major works for a hydro power project. Natural calamities manifesting in unprecedented floods, landslides, earthquakes, geological surprises etc. prove to be the deterimental to smooth execution of project. Very recently, severe landslides in Doyang project has caused power house flooding and serious damages to other civil structures at the final stage of execution, thereby delaying the commissioning schedule substantially. However, proper construction planning and efforts to minimise the damages caused by *such force majure* conditions may remove such impediments to a great extent.

Facilities to the Contractors

Inadequate provision of consruction power and other resources committed to the contractors, improper roads and communication facilities, non-orchestrated works taken up by different contractors leading to lack of co-ordination and blockade of one's work by poor performance of the other(s) etc. are some of the major hindrances to the smooth implementation of hydro power projects. Due care by the project authorities may reduce the delay associated with these factors.

Improper Documentation

Maintaining proper documentation of past observations, experiences, actions and causes of past 'time and cost over runs' of power projects and continuation of collection of important hydrometeorological, instrumentation and other data, even after completion of a project is vital not only for future development of hydro power in the region, but also for taking up renovation and modernisation of the existing project. Lack of such record is a drawback and due care needs to be taken in this regard.

Conclusion

The river systems of the North Eastern Region of India possesses huge potential of hydro power resource. In order to achieve economy and optimality in power generation in a grid system by generating hydro electric power, development of hydro power potential of the rivers in the region needs special attention. Inherent advantages of hydro power development need to be highlighted to remove any apprehension and misconception against such development. The bottlenecks which are likely to impede the process of hydro power development need identification and concerted efforts in right earnest by all concerned need to be put to translate the high prospect of hydro power development in the river basins of the region into reality.

REFERENCES

Proceedings on the "Conference on Hydro Power Development — Issues, Challenges and Opportunities" held during 24-25 April 1997 organised by CBIP and co-organised by Society of Power Engineers (India).

Irrigation and Power Journal, Golden Jubilee Issue, January, 1994 by CBIP.

Basic Statistics of North Eastern Region 1995 by North Eastern Council.

Annual Report of NEREB for the year 1996-97.

System Status Report of N.E. Region by PGCI for the Month of April, 1998.

Technical Bulletin of the Seminar of Development and Conservation of Energy Resources in North Eastern India, conducted during 7-8 Jan., 1984 by the Institution of Engineers (I) Assam State Centre.

"Geology for Engineers" by D. S. Arora.

Fifteenth Electric Power Survey of India July 1995 by Central Electricity Authority.

Major causes of Time and Cost Overrun of Hydro Electric Projects and Remedial Actions — A Study done at New Delhi Design Office of NEEPCO.

Morphological Studies of the River Brahmaputra prepared by the WAPCOS(I) Ltd. for the Brahmaputra Board.

PART-II

CASE STUDIES

3

BRAHMAPUTRA RIVER AND PROSPECTIVE DEVELOPMENT OF ASSAM

A. K. BORA

Brahmaputra is one of the resourceful river of the world. Its 640 km long course within Assam has created the extensive fertile alluvial plains which were and still continue to be the cradle of the Brahmaputra Valley civilization. Though historically the valley has been variably inundated by the Brahmaputra floods, the present flood problem has assumed serious proportions causing damage to all sectors of Assam's economy. But, the proper utilization of its vast water resources for the development of hydel power, irrigation and navigation, and the management of flood through floodplain zoning and perusing the concept of living with floods for averting the risk of flood damage have been considered the key factors for economic development of Assam. This paper attempts to outline the ways the resourceful Brahmaputra may be utilised for the overall development of Assam.

The Brahmaputra is one of the largest rivers of the world. It forms a vast and complex river system (Fig. 3.1) characterised by the most dynamic and unique water and sediment transport pattern. The Brahmaputra is the fourth largest river in the world in terms of average discharge at the mouth with a flow of 19,830 $m^{-3}s^{-1}$. As regards sediment transport, the river has also set records in carrying

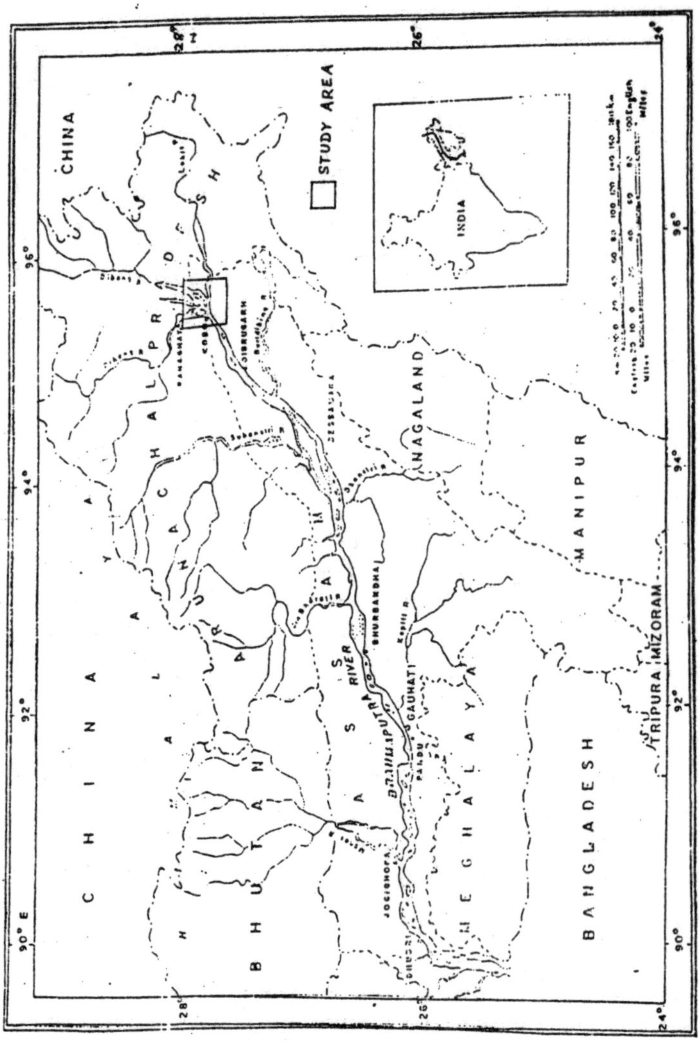

Fig. 3.1: The Brahmputra River System in Assam

alarming volume of sediments. The high intensity of monsoonal rains, easily erodible rocks, steep slopes and high seismicity contribute a lot by rendering the river a heavily sediment-laden one. Thus, the Brahmaputra becomes one of the leading sediment carrying rivers of the world. It is second only to the Yellow river of China in the amount of sediment transported per unit of drainage area. At Pandu (Guwahati), the river carries an average annual suspended load of 402 million metric tonnes (Goswami, 1985). A river with such gigantic water and sediment discharge magnitudes represents its most dynamic fluival regime. Its large alluvial channel having a width of 6 to 10 km is marked by intense braiding, rapid aggradation and drastic bankline changes. Besides, the river creates severe flood hazards and untold miseries to the people of Assam with its recurrent deluging floods. The recurring floods of characteristically high magnitudes have assumed devastating dimensions heavily affecting the agricultural lands, crops, cattles and people and above all the agrarian economy of the state (Bhattacharyya and Bora, 1997). In view of the growing extent of inundation and increasing quantum of flood damages, there is an overriding need to launch some eco-friendly flood management plans to control floods and reduce flood damages. With plenty of water resources the Brahmaputra river bears immense prospect for achieving prosperous development in all fronts of Assam's and North East India's economies (Bora, 1999).

Water Resources Development Prospect

The Brahmaputra valley of Assam by virtue of its unique geographical location and humid tropical monsoon climate happens to be a land of innumerable rivers and tributaries. Due to favourable natural factors, especially the slope, physiography and heavy monsoon rains, the Brahmaputra and its tributaries bear abundant water resources thereby offering great prospect for hydro power generation. The Brahmaputra river system carries a tremendous hydro power potential which remains almost untapped till today. The entire annual runoff of 50 million hectare metres, measured on the Brahmaputra at Pandu (Guwahati) goes waste into the Bay of

Bengal. As per the survey conducted by the Central Water and Power Commission, the Brahmaputra basin has the hydro electric power potential of 34,920 kW at 60 per cent load factor which is about 41.5 per cent, i.e., two-fifth of the country's total hydro-electric potential of 84,044 MW. Excluding the sub-basins of the Brahmaputra falling outside the north-eastern region, the basin represents hydro power potential of 31,857 MW (at 60 per cent load factor) accounting for 38 per cent of the counry's total potential. The enormity of hydro power potential of the Brahmaputra is thus quite evident from these statistics. It is an emphatic yes that this mega amount of power, if generated would boost up the economy of Assam as well as North East India. Besides, home consumption, the surplus may also be exported and sold to the neighbouring countries for earning crores of rupees. But, it is regrettable that despite having vast hydro-power potential, only a nominal fraction of 600 MW i.e., only 1.88 per cent is so far harnessed. As regards the utilisation level of the Brahmaputra's runoff, the fact represents a more dismal picture in the context of the other Indian rivers (Table 3.1). Out of the total runoff of 1853.5 cubic km for Indian rivers, the Brahmaputra carries an average annual runoff of 627.87 cubic km i.e., 33.87 per cent of India's total. But only 0.07 per cent of the Brahmaputra runoff is utilised so far as water storage for hydel power generation is concerned.

Table 3.1 : India's River Runoff and Utilisation Level

River Basins	*Average Annual Runoff (cubic km)*	*Per cent of India's total*	*Water storage*	
			cubic km.	*Percent of utilisation*
1. Ganges	501.64	27.06	32.20	6.42
2. Brahmaputra	627.87	33.87	0.47	0.07
3. Godavari	118.98	6.42	18.55	15.59
4. Mahanadi	66.88	3.60	8.31	12.42
5. Narmada	40.95	2.21	2.80	6.83
6. Brahmoni & Baitarani	36.23	1.95	1.08	2.98
India's Total	1853.50	100.00	143.02	7.72

However, the nominal hydro power development in the Brahmaputra basin may be attributed to a number of problems like the inter-state disputes and hindrances such as adverse geological conditions, high seismicity, difficult terrains and peculiar land-holding systems in the hill states of the North East India. The granting of statehood has aggravated the inter-state disputes over the sharing of water resources of the Brahmaputra tributaries. This has led to abandonment of some good projects before being completed and implemented. But, the states falling in the Brahmaputra basin should realise that they can earn high amount of revenue from hydro power generation than that from the exploitation of forest resources (Bora, 1999). Water power is a green power which is obtained from non-polluting source with high conversion efficiency. Therefore, instead of large scale exploitation and destruction of forest resources for revenue earning which has more adverse ecological impact, the north eastern states should reorient their attitude and give more emphasis on harnessing the vast water resources for sustainable economic development. However, the scale of the hydro power development projects should be considered in view of seismic aspect of the region. The North Eastern Region falls in a high frequency earthquake prone zone. As the entire Himalayan foothill belt providing most favourable hydro power generation dam sites is notorious for high seismicity and frequent incidence of landslides, large dams are no way risk free. But, it is rue that vast water resources must be developed and the furry of floods needs to be reduced. So, it is advisable that the small and medium scale water resource development options taking the major tributaries of the Brahmaputra into consideration should receive due attetnion. Of course, some hydro power projects on certain tributary rivers have been proposed (Table 3.2). If the dam projects like Dihang and Subansiri are implemented, the flood-level of the Brahmaputra is expected to go down by 1-2 m and 0.25-0.6 m respectively due to these two projects besides hydel power generation.

Besides, being used for hydel power generation, the water resources of the river may be largely utilised for irrigational purposes. In order to produce more foodgrains as demanded by

Table 3.2 : Proposed Dam Projects and Hydel Power Potential in the Brahmaputra Valley

Dam Projects	*Potential Hydel Power (MW)*
1. Dihang	20,000 (F. L. down to 1-2 m)
2. Manas	5,000
3. Subansiri	4,800 (F.L. down to 0.25-0.6 m)
4. Lohit	3,000
5. Dibong	2,500
6. Jia Baharali	2,000
7. Sonkosh	1,500
8. Damoi	1,000
9. Kameng	600

explosive growth of population in Assam, creation of irrigation potential is a viable alternative. The State of Assam as may generally be conceived needs no or very little artificial supply of water for its agriculture. But, a close observation of the prevailing agro-climatic conditions of the State well ascertains the necessity of irrigation more particularly during the rabi crop season. In the predominantly traditional agrarian and monsoon dominated lands of Assam, where winter cropping is difficult due to lack of rain water, irrigation plays a decisive role in respect of number of crops raised during an agricultural year. But, the intensity of irrigation in the state is far below the level of expectation. It is disheartening to note that the gross irrigated area in Assam constitutes only 15.06 per cent of the state's gross cropped area. But, there is tremendous prospect for substantial development in agricultural production, if the Brahmaputra's vast water resources are properly utilised in irrigating the fertile crop lands.

Flood Management

Flood in Assam has become a recurring feature since early times. The Brahmaputra valley of Assam has been variably inundated by the frequent flood of high magnitudes. Brahmaputra river system is so vast, and geo-physically and hydrologically so dynamic that its natural processes and factors alone are adequate to cause devastating floods in the narrow valley (Bora, 2001). In most of the cases, the natural and hydro-meteorological factors including the heavy monsoonal rains, frequent landslides coupled with easy erodibility of rocks, steep slopes and high seismicity constitute the major causes of Brahmaputra floods. High intensity of rainfall accounting for about 70 per cent of the total annual rainfall occurring during the summer months of June to September obviously becomes capable of creating unbelievable fresh floods in the valley. Seismic and geologic factors also aggravate the flood situation. The great earthquakes of 1897 and 1950 caused notable changes in the fluvial regime of the valley by suddenly raising the river beds. The aggradation of river beds due to silting has forced the rivers to spill their water overbank, inundating large tracts of land in the valley. The severe floods of 1954, 1955, 1956 and 1958 occurring immediately after the 1950 earthquake are the daring examples. Besides, the natural factors, the human-induced factors are also highly responsible for devastating floods in Assam. Deforestation and unwise tree felling in the hills and foothills, large scale human encroachment upon the floodplain, destruction of wetlands and the poorly managed embankment network are highly responsible for increasing frequency of floods and quantum of damages in the Brahmaputra valley.

The recurring floods of characteristically high magnitudes have assumed devastating dimensions heavily affecting the agricultural lands, crops, people and cattles and above all the agrarian economy of the State. As regards flood damages in the Brahmaputra valley, the frequency and time of flood occurrence are of great significance. The valley commonly receives severe floods of different occurring at least 4-5 times in a year. Normally, about 40 pcr cent area of the valley is affected by flood. The valley presently accounts for about 7.5 per cent of the total flood damaged area in India and represents nearly 2 per cent of the total damage caused. The flood damage data available for the Brahmaputra valley indicates that the cropped area damaged and number of affected people are gradually increased during the period 1954-98 (Table 3.3). Among the years 1988 has been recognised as the year of most severe flood occurring in four waves.

In view of the growing extent of inundation and inceasing quantum of flood damages over the years, there is an overriding need to launch some eco-friendly and properly planned flood management activities in the Brahmaputra valley.

Table 3.3 : Flood Damages during Major Floods in the Brahmaputra Valley

Year of Major floods	*No. of flood waves*	*Area affected (mha)*	*Cropped area damaged (mha)*	*Population affected (m)*
1954	4	2.90	0.30	1.30
1955	—	1.35	0.07	0.18
1958	—	1.23	0.06	0.40
1962	2	1.59	0.36	3.91
1966	4	1.51	0.06	3.62
1972	2	1.01	0.36	2.95
1973	—	2.31	0.17	1.84
1977	3	1.02	NA*	4.54
1980	—	1.14	0.26	3.35
1984	4	1.49	0.14	5.61
1987	—	1.62	0.43	NA*
1988	4	3.82	1.12	8.31
1993	—	1.25	0.22	5.30
1996	—	1.33	0.28	5.12
1998	3	0.97	0.29	4.69

* NA stands for not available.

Experts now agreed that complete conrol of flood of the Brahmaputra is not at all feasible. Floods, to a certain degree, will continue to occur as their casual factors are of both natural and human-induced origin. So, it is quite appropriate to pursue the concept of flood management rather than the concept of flood control. Floodplain zoning and management is the effective way of moderating floods and reducing hazards. The basic concept of floodplain zoning involves regulating the land use in the floodplain with a view to restricting the flood damages. Effective floodplain zoning is the only way to minimise the flood loss. But, the present floodplain management scenario in the Brahmaputra valley is indeed a dismal one. In recent years, large scale encroachment of the floodplain and the low lying areas for habitation and cultivation has created acute flood problem. Similarly, the destruction of wet lands and swamps has also added a new dimension to the cause and effect of flooding. Thus, the human use of the floodplain should be regulated by identifying the risk zones and appropriate flood management programmes can be carried out in these zones by the concerned government departments. But, the management of floodplain and reduction of flood hazards need to be approached through properly planned and designed flood management activities.

Historically, the people of Assam are well acquainted with floods and spontaneously they have acquired the art of living with floods to a considerable extent. But, in the recent years, floods of the Brahmaputra with their high magnitudes and frequencies have appeared to be greatly hazardous to the floodplain dwellers. In view of the increasing trend in flood damage in the valley, it can be realised that the measures so far adopted for flood control are totally inadequate in proportion to the dimension of the Brahmaputra flood problem. So, there is an imperative need to pursue the approach of "living with floods". Otherwise, the people living in the floodplain would suffer severely from recurring floods and for many, particularly the poor peasants, there is no alternative but to cultivate the land and accept the risk and loss. In fact, the present human adjustment to Brahmaputra floods is certainly of "accepting the loss type". The approach of living with floods is thought to be much more effective in averting the risk of flood damage in the valley. The extent of flood damage primarily depends on the time of their occurrence. Unfortunately, the main cropping season, i.e., the summer cultivation season or paddy season from June to August in the valley coincides with the period of intense monsoonal activity and resultant floods. As a result, the floods occurring during June-September have the most devastating effect on agriculture. The cropping system in the valley, therefore, has to be scientifically adapted to the rhythm of regular flooding. To this effect, a suitable and appropriate crop calendar should be evolved keeping in mind that possible floods may substantially reduce crop damage. In the chronically flood affected areas, summer cropping should thus be substituted by large scale winter cropping.

Conclusion

The Brahmaputra being a resourceful river is the life line of Assam as well as North East India. The river bears immense hydro power potential accoutning for 38 per cent of the country's total potential. In spite of the vast water resources of the river with substantial hydro power potential which is only nominally harnessed so far for power generation and least used for irrigation, about an annual runoff of 50 million hectare meters (measured at Pandu, Guwahati) go waste into the Bay of Bengal. Being charged with high volume of water, the river, in turn has been causing havoc in its valley by inundating and eroding large areas. The economy of Assam has been greatly impaired by recurring flood loss in the agricultural sector. Unless the vast water resources of the river are properly harnessed and utilised and the floods are moderated, no sector of Assam's economy, be it agriculture, energy, communication or industry is going to sustain in future.

REFERENCES

Bhattacharyya, N.N. and Bora, A.K. (1997) *Floods of the Brahmaputra River in India,* Water Internatinoal, IWRA, University of New Maxico, U.S.A., Vol. 22, No. 4.

Bora, A.A. (1999). *Drainage and Flood of Assam* in Bhagabati, A.K., Bora, A.K. and Kar, K. edited *Geography of Assam,* Rajesh Publications, New Delhi, 36-51.

Bora, A.A. (1999). Hydro Power Development in the North East, *The Assam Tribune,* Guwahati, February 29.

Goswami, D.C. (1985). Brahmaputra River, Assam, India; Physiography, Basin Denundation and Channel Aggradation, Water Resources Research, 21, 959-978.

4

STEAMER GHATS (FERRY GHATS) OF BRAHMAPUTRA RIVER : Impact on Region's Economy and Environment

B. SAIKIA and P. DAS

Flowing across the State, the mighty river, Brahmaputra offers immense opportunities for the development of inland water transport in Assam. The whole southern part of the region along with the five neighbouring states has the link wih the rest of the country through this river. From this point of view, the development of water transport system particularly steamer ghats (Ferry Ghats) along the river banks is essential.

The study is based mainly on secondary data collected from various sources to access the number and volume of passengers and cargos. Some primary information has also been collected from the field. Besides, personal interviews, maps and Cartographic methods are used to make the study a significant one.

INTRODUCTION

Brahmaputra river originates in a great glacier mass in Kailas Range of the Himalayas, South of lake Gunkyud in South West Tibet (Elevation : 5300 m) and flows through China, India and Bangladesh for a total distance of 2880 km. It finally debouches into Bay of Bengal. In India, it flows through Arunachal and Assam. More than 100 tributaries of North and South contribute water to Brahmaputra which covers 1.75 lakh sq. km. area of whole of North East India. The average width of the channel is 8 km and average gradient is 13 cm/km. (Taher, 1988). It is the 4th largest river in terms of average discharge at mouth (19,820 m^3/sec) and 2nd largest in terms of sediment transported per unit drainage area. The Brahmaputra valley in Assam section is 720 km long and 80-90 km. wide.

Significance of the Study

(i) The river Brahmaputra serves as a great highway of trade and commerce and inland transport which ultimately help all round development of the region.

(ii) Water transport is cheaper than land transport because it provides readymade highways. There is no capital outlay for construction and maintenance like road transport.

(iii) For the movement of bulky goods (Coal, Petroleum, Iron ore) to foreign countries water transport is indispensable and advantageous than road and air transport.

(iv) It provides promotion of internal trade and commerce.

(v) It is environment friendly (sound and air pollution being quite low).

(vi) Inland waterways serves two functions :

   (a) Transportation to and from Ocean ports.

   (b) Transportation between important producing districts within the country or state.

(vii) The southern part of Brahmaputra valley along with other N.E. States have link with India across the river Brahmaputra.

For these reasons, the development of water transport i.e. Steamer/Ferry ghats across the river is essential and significant.

History of Development of Steamer Ferry Ghats in Assam

From the very early times Assam's trade with the neighbouring provinces was mainly carried by river transport, the main route to Bengal, Bihar and Orissa being the Brahmaputra and Ganges.

In 1839, when the Assam Company was formed, it started its own fleet of country boats. In 1844, the river journey from Guwahati to Sadiya started by country boats (which took 6 weeks). Until 1847 the chief mode of transport in Assam was country boats.

In 1847 the Steamer service was established in Brahmaputra between Calcutta and Guwahati. During 1856, the Government Steamer service was extended from Guwahati to Dibrugarh. In 1861 the IGSN (Indian General Steam Navigation) and in 1862 the RSN (River Steam Navigation) companies started regular traffic operation on the Brahmaputra. During 1905 daily steamer service was started between Dhubri and Guwahati in both directions.

After the partition of 1947, the RSN and IGSN companies obtained monopoly of traffic (Tea/Jute) between Calcutta and Assam directly. J.S. Company (Private) was most busy in transportation of goods before 1949 (opening of railway) which continued operating upto 1967. Two Public Sector Organisations viz., the State Directorate of Inland Water Transport (IWT, 1959) and the Central Inland Water Transport Corporation (CIWTC, 1967) are presently operating water transport services in the State on commercial basis since 1959 and 1967 respectively. There were 43 ferry services in Assam during 1992-93 which rose to 72 at present among which about 15 services were very important (Fig. 4.1). These are listed in Table 4.1

Table 4.1 : Important Ferry Services of Assam

Sl. No.	*Important Ferry Services*
1.	Dhubri — Fakirganj
2.	Jogighopa — Pancharatna — Goalpara
3.	Baghbar — Goalpara
4.	Sontoli — Bohori
5.	Guwahati — North Guwahati
6.	Guwahati — Raja duar
7.	Guwahati — Kurua
8.	Tezpur — Lawkhowa
9.	Dhansiri — Gomiri
10.	Neamati — Kamalabari
11.	Desangnmukh — Matmora
12.	Dibru — Sissi
13.	Dibru — Sonari
14.	Sadiaya — Saikhowaghat
15.	(a) Singri — Dhing
	(b) Silghat — Panpur
	(c) Tezpur — Burhachapari

Source : Director of Inland Water Transport, Assam

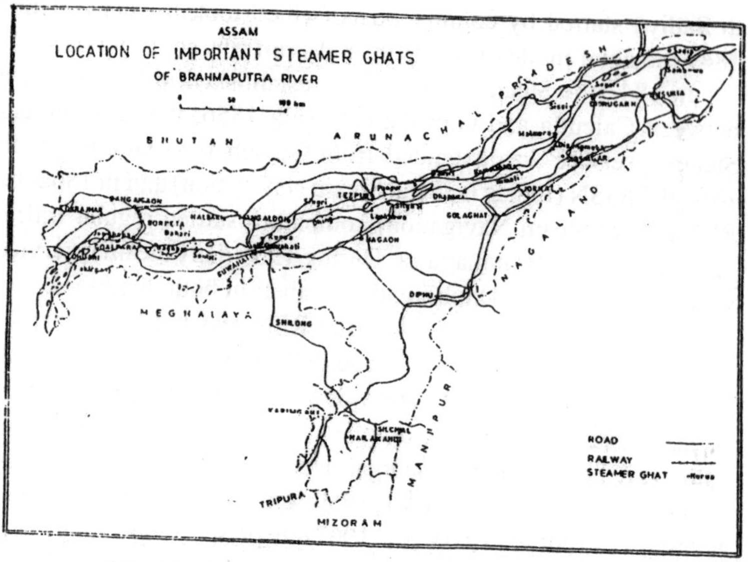

Fig. 4.1 : Assam : Location of Important Steamer Ghats

There were 10 Ramp Powered Light Vessels (Less than 80 tonnes) 34 Modern Steel Vessels (45-80 tonnes), 17 Marboats (18 tonnes), 58 Single boats (1-10 tonnes), 9 Pantoons and 4 Relief boats (5 or more than 5 tonnes) during 1993-94 in Assam.

These vessels carried huge amount of passengers and cargoes which has pointed out the necessity of IWT system in the river Brahmaputra.

Methodology

The study is based mainly on secondary data collected from Director of IWT, Assam to assess the amount and volume of passengers and cargoes. Different published works have been consulted for this regard. Statistical Handbook, Assam; Economic Survey, Assam; Gazetteer of India, Assam State, Darrang District; Geographical Journals (NEIGS) are taken into consideration for this regard. Some primary information has also been collected from the fields. Besides, personal interviews, maps and cartographic methods are taken into account to make the study a significant one. The location of ferry ghats of Brahmaputra river alongwith roadways and railways are shown in a map of Assam from which we can know the co-ordination of modes of transport. Histograms are drawn to compare the passengers, cargoes, vehicles and animals carried by IWT system during different periods.

In order to show the impact and significance of ferry ghats on region's economy and environment some objectives are taken. The objectives are cofined mainly to the examination of—

- (i) The amount of passengers and volume of cargoes carried through these ghats;
- (ii) The nature and extent of movement of cargos;
- (iii) The role of ferry ghats in developing various centres in either side of the river;
- (iv) The economic importance of IWT system for regional development and
- (v) The impact of IWT system on society and environment.

Firstly, mention may be made about the amount of passengers and volume of cargoes carried through these ghats. Before 1847, movement of passengers and cargoes were performed mainly by country boats between Assam and Calcutta. During 1847 when steamer service started in Brahmaputra between Guwahati and Calcutta it became more profitable and suitable for the export and import of valuable items like opium, liquor, coal, cotton, piece goods, Iron ore, railway plants (Import item) and ivory, tea, wax, rubber (export item). Before 1949 (Assam Rail Link Establishment) the J.S Companies carried about 80 per cent of the tea, 90 per cent of Jute and large volume of Petroleum products from Assam to Calcutta till 1963-64 and also moved in large volume of imports. Inland Water Transport Committee (1959) stated that during this period 93 per cent of total tea poduction and 90 per cent of Jute crops were exported by river transport from Assam. During 1965, goods and traffic carried by J.S. Companies were in the order of 1,96,919 tonnes of import items and 1,17,313 tonnes of exports.

Cargoes and passengers handled by ferries in Assam during different periods are given for comparison in Table 4.2

Table 4.2 : Cargoes and Passengers handled by Ferries in different years, Assam

Years	*Passengers*	*Cargo (Tonnes)*	*Vehicles (H/C Scooter/bicycle)*	*Animals*
1975-76	24,35,219	27,632	14,951	72,015
1983-84	25,00,000	41,800	89,000	24,000
1992-93	60,12,000	96,447	7,70,986	58,121

Source : Director of Inland Water Transport, Assam.

During 1992-93, the vessels of IWT carried on an average 16,471 passengers and 264 tonnes of goods per day. This huge volume of traffic has pointed out the necessity of IWT system in Brahmaputra. Figure 4.2 will give a general idea regarding its importance in Assam.

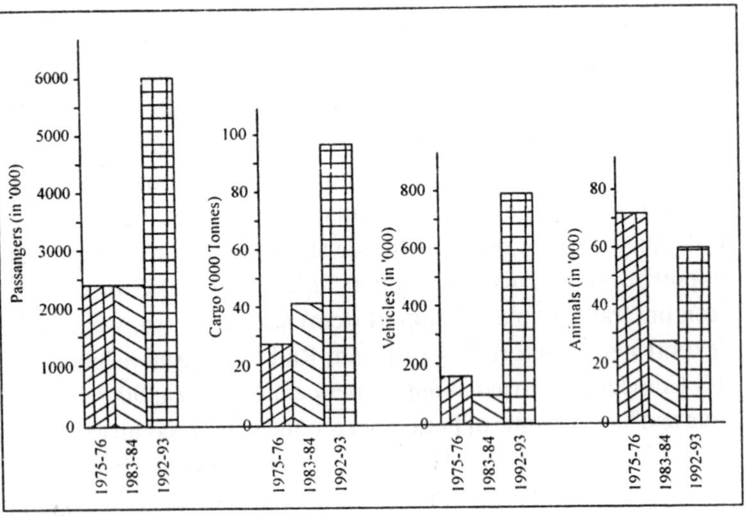

Fig. 4.2 : Cargo and Passengers handled by the Ferries

Secondly, it can be viewed that the nature of goods were bulky and less valuable which were carried by country boats and steamers as well. From the very early times Assam's trade with neighbouring provinces was mainly carried by river transport. From Assam to Bengal, Bihar and Orissa the main routes were Brahmaputra and Ganges. Until 1847 the chief mode of transport was country boat but after 1847 it was steamer service. Boat transportation on Brahmaputra was not reliable because of long and tedius journey. Main import items by boat were kerosene, sugar, tobacco, dry fish, lime, rice etc. Due to less transport cost the more bulky and less valuable commodities like paddy, raw cotton, timber, jute, mustard, hides were exported by boats from Assam to Bengal.

Import items to Assam by steamer includes valuable commodities like opium, liquor, coal, cotton piece goods, metal, railway plants, etc. Export by steamer includes ivory, tea, wax, rubber, raw silk from Assam to Calcutta and Bangladesh. The steamer service was found from Assam to Calcutta, Bihar, Orissa and Bangladesh. Guwahati has ferry services with Dibrugarh, Dhubri, Sadiya and other centres which carry different agricultural and industrial products.

Thirdly, the various centres have been growing in either side of the river on the basis of different steamer ghats e.g. from Dhubri in the west to Dibrugarh in the east many centres have been growing. These are Dhubri (Match factory), Jogighopa (Ashok Paper Mill), Goalpara, Pancharatna, Guwahati, North Guwahati, Amingaon, Tezpur, Silghat, Burachapari, Nematighat, Kamalabari, Majulyu and Dibrugarh.

Fourthly, IWT system plays a greater role for region's economic development. In this context some examples may be cited —

(a) Burhachapari which is located just opposite to Tezpur Ferrighat supplied enormous amount of milk and vegetables daily to Tezpur through this ghat which helps the people of both the regions economically. Burhachapari is growing mainly depending on the vast market of Tezpur town which has a population of 55,000 (1991).

(b) Prior to the construction of Kaliabhomora Bridge (1987) the Silghat Jute Mill was established (1970) on southern bank of the river on the basis of Tezpur Silghat Ferry ghat.

Silghat Ferry ghat helps this industry in terms of collections of raw jute and despatching its products to other areas.

(c) Likewise, Jogighopa Paper Mill which was established during 1970s taking advantage of ferry ghats of Jogighopa for collecting and distributing their goods.

(d) For Dhubri Match Factory, the necessary raw materials (Simul tree) are entirely collected through this waterway which is significant for the development of the region economically.

(e) Majuli, the world's largest river island entirely depended on the ferry ghats of the either side for its reginoal economic development. Majuli has ferry connections with Neamatighat in the south and Bodotighat in the north and by these ghats it is connected with other parts of Assam. It is important to note that Majuli has a greater significance as a centre of Baishnavite culture.

(f) The Government of Assam received Rs. 56,24,000 as revenue from the ferry ghats, by handling passengers, cargoes, vehicles and animals during 1992-93. During 1997 the IWT system collected an amount of Rs. 2.47 crore as revenue which was much better in comparison to 1996 figure. This ultimately helps in the region's economic development.

(g) North bank and South bank *Char* economy (Island economy) is well connected by these ferry ghats which helps exchange of goods between *Char* (Islands) and ultimately helps in the development of the *Char* areas economically.

(h) The "riverine landscape" is an important attraction to the tourist. Extension of ferry services in the Brahmaputra may therefore help in boosting tourism in the State, thereby enhancing its economy.

(i) The last but not the least is that Dibrugarh, the major town of Upper Assam is located just near the southern bank of Brahmaputra. Since the British period, Dibrugarh was connected with other parts through Brahmaputra. It was grown as an urban centre due to the production of oil and tea in surrounding areas.

Finally, the IWT system has great impact on society and environment as well. For example, the largest river island Majuli is grown for well developed waterways through Brahmaputra. A distinctive type of culture is observed among the people of Majuli e.g. Baishnavite culture, growth of many *Satras* which are not commonly found in other areas.

Before the construction of Bhomoraguri Bridge there were good socio-cultural links (marriages, etc.) among he people of Nowgong and Sonitpur Districts. This was possible only because of good ferry services connecting these two districts. Thus cultural assimilation takes place through ferry services.

Other newly emerged river islands (*Chars*) like Burhachapari and Lawkhowa Chapari (Sonitpur District) have separate types of society. These are purely agricultural societies and their day-to-day lives are dependent on these ghats.

The whole North East India depends on road transport system and the region becomes detached frequently during rainy season by the overflowing of tributaries. On the other hand, the region is affected by frequent floods each and every year which causes interruption in road and rail transport system. The whole region then suffers from natural economic blockade for which the society suffers a lot. At the same time construction and maintenance of roads become expensive and dificult here. In view of this ferry service can be utilised as an alternative mode of transport. Employment opportunities become more if water transport system is developed.

The IWT system has great impact directly or indirectly on the environment, for example —

(i) The North East states as a whole, are mainly depended on the road transport, the transportation of huge volume of carriable goods can also be made posible through waterways. Transportation of goods by road transport causes enhancement in the rate of traffic flow which is now considered as a major factor for environmental pollution. On the other hand, the water transport system provides uninterrupted service of transhipment, which is comparatively low fuel consuming system. Therefore, it saves the pollution as well as the most valuable exhaustible energy resource i.e. fossil fuel.

(ii) Secondly, water transport is environment friendly in the sense that it is comparatively free from sound and air pollution and at the same time water transport has less accident risk as compared to roads and railways.

Conclusion and Suggestion

From the above discussion it is clear that the IWT system has great influence on the region's economic, social and environmental aspect. It has a positive impact on region's development. It is felt that construction of new bridges over Brahmaputra has reduced the importance of ferry ghats to some extent. So, special measures should be taken for proper development of IWT system.

The problem generally faced by the IWT system in the Brahmaputra river is heavy siltation and fluctuation in water level which can be solved by dredging the bed of the river at certain localities wherever it becomes necessary. This can raise the efficiency of transport.

Introduction of technically more efficient machineries in IWT will enhance the efficiency of service which will attract more passengers and cargoes.

The *Chars* and *Chaparies* (river islands) should be well connected with frequent service by the modern ferries. By this process the poor peasants can carry their agricultural products quickly and easily to the nearby market centres which in turn will help economic and regional development of the *Chars* and *Chaparies*. Because, at present most of the *Chars* and *Chaparies* are connected by small country boats.

Necessary formalities (treaty) should be obtained with Bangladesh Government to open up the water ways upto Bay of Bengal so that this North East region can be connected with the neighbouring regions both inside and outside the country.

Recently, Central Government has given proper emphasis to develop this national waterway with a view to build a healthy economic environment in whole of South East Asia for the purpose of extending trade and commerce in this region.

It is learned that the State Government has submitted a proposal to the Centre seeking an amount of Rs. 122 crores for modernisation and expansion of the IWT Department with an intention for replacement and modernisation of existing ferry services, boost tourism by introducing luxury vessels from Guwahati to Kaziranga, Umananda and Doul-Govinda. Moreover, the State Government is planning to set up a Research and Analysis wing and to develop the Crew Training Centre (CWC).

Night service should also be introduced in ferry ghats to enhance its efficiency.

For Brahmaputra river, sufficient gauge discharge data is not available. If ferry services are increased in different points, and the persons engaged in the ferries be trained properly, then it will help for getting abundant gauge discharge data for different stations. This will help in running the ferries as well as for taking adequate flood protection measures. This will raise the employment opportunity of the persons to be engaged in ferries and also lessen the allotment of money in this field.

The Northern Brahmaputra plain is socio-economically less developed than that of the Southern one. The ferry service connecting these two plains may bring about a balanced development or in other words may remove regional inequalities to a great extent.

REFERENCES

Dutta, N.C., (1978), *Assam District Gazetteer,* Darrang, District, Government Press, Assam, Guwahati.

Economic Survey, Assam, 1973-74 and 1989-90, Directorate of Economic and Statistics, Government of Assam, Guwahati.

Hussain, M. (1994), *Transport Geography* (ed.) Anmol Publication Pvt. Ltd., New Delhi.

Medni, S.B. (1978), *Transport System and Economic Development in Assam,* Publication Board of Assam, Guwahati.

Statistical Handbook, Assam, 1994, Directorate of Economics and Statistics, Government of Assam, Guwahati.

Taher, Dr. M. (1988), *Geography of North-East India,* El-Dorado Publication, Srimantapur, Guwahati.

5

JIA-DHANSIRI IRRIGATION PROJECT
Impact on Agricultural Development in Darrang District

CHARU SAHARIA (NATH)

INTRODUCTION

The Darrang District, which is situated in the middle part of Assam, is constituted by two sub-divisions — Managaldai and Udalguri. It is located between the latitudes of 26°9′ N and 26°52′ N and longitudes of 91°45′ E and 92°22′ E. The region covers an alluvial tract between the river Brahmaputra on the south and the foothills of the Bhutan and Arunachal Himalayas on the north. The total geographical area of the region is 3465.30 sq. km. with a population of 1286633 in 1991. The district of Darrang is surrounded by Bhutan and Arunachal Pradesh on the north, Sonitpur district on the east, Marigaon and Kamrup district on the south and Kamrup district on the west. There are six development blocks in the region. Four new development blocks are declared at present in addition to these six development blocks. For convenience of study, the district has been divided into six blocks.

Physiographically the district of Darrang is a part of the Brahmaputra river valley. It lies between the Himalayas on the north and the southern bank of the Brahmaputra on the south.

The mighty river Brahmaputra is flowing from east to west through the southern part of the district. The general slope of the land surface of the district is from north to south towards the Brahmaputra. Almost all the tributaries and the stream rising in the Himalayas flow from North to South towards the river.

The river Jia-Dhansiri is one of the important tributaries of the Brahmaputra. It originates from Bhutan hills and flow through the east of Rowta and through whole of eastern boundary of Dalgaon Sialmari block and also through Udalguri and Majbat development block. Its approximate length is about 80 km from its source to outfall. The river is of very little importance in the hills but grows in size and importance when it enters the valley being fed by other streams. Due to shallowness in the lower reaches, it has a tendency to change its course, specially, during the flood season causing havoc to human life and property. The most severe floods occur when very heavy rainfall takes place simultaneously in different parts of the river basin.

The river has a steep bed slope in the upper reaches and assumes a flat slope as it enters the plains. The slope of the bed is very flat near the confluence with the Brahmaputra. The slope of the bed in the last 29 km between the railway bridge and its confluence is 1.25 metre per km (Dutta, 1978). Rapid siltation and erosion take place in the lower reaches of the river.

The total irrigated area of the district was 38,557 hectares or 14.16 per cent of the total cropped area in the district (Fig. 5.1). There are some minor irrigation projects in the district. The major project of river Jia Dhansiri at Bhairabkhuda is located about 20 kms north of Udalguri. The irrigation project has remained incomplete, but it irrigates about 5,500 hectares of cultivated area of the district. The project covers a part of Udalguri block.

Significance

A study on impact of Dhansiri Irrigation Project on Agricultural Development in Darrang District, Assam is important and useful, because, this is the major irrigation project of the district. It is necessary to study the agricultural development in an area and also the impact of associated irrigation projects, so that the agricultural

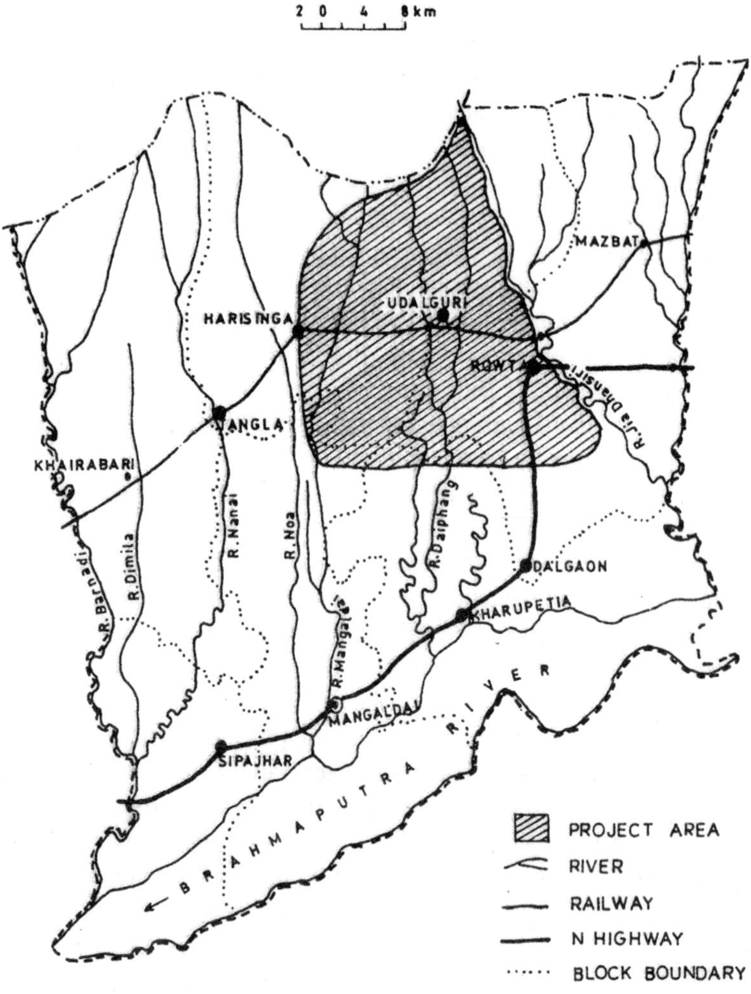

Fig. 5.1 : Darrang District : Area under Dhansiri Irrigation Project

planners and policy makers may be careful and can take necessary steps for better development of agriculture.

Methodology

For this study several methods and tools are used. Primary data are collected from 20 per cent of the villages of the effected area. Secondary data are collected from the District Gazetteer, District Irrigation Office and Census Handbook. The land utilization and productive behaviour of the people are studied through collection of secondary data. The data and informations are processed, tabulated and analysed using thematic maps and graphs.

Objectives

The main objectives of the study are :

1. to examine the impact of Dhansiri Irrigation Project over the development of agriculture in the district.
2. to analyse the agricultural land use pattern and productivity in the district.
3. to elicit the problems associated with the development of agricultural productivity.

Population Structure

In 1991, the population structure of the district was as follows : immigrant Muslims 2,53,681 (22.22%); indigenous tribal 2,07,490 (17.63%); indigenous non-tribal 4,83,768 (41.71%); immigrant Hindu refugees 84,274 (7.52%); Nepalese 42,440 (3.66%); ex-tea garden labourers and adibasis 67.923 (5.86%) and others 16,284 (1.4%). The immigrant Muslims constituted absolute majority in two blocks (Majbat and Dalgaon Sialmari). Their numbers were more than 97 per cent in each of these blocks, whereas most of the people of Udalguri block belonged to scheduled tribes category.

Irrigation and Agricultural Landuse

Irrigation is indeed the life breath of agriculture. It is already known that rainfall in the district of Darrang is erratic and unpredictable varying from 8.7 mm to 488.2 mm per month. The total seasonal rainfall during winter months, i.e., from Dcember to February varies from 16.8 to 68.8 mm in the district. Rainfall during pre-monsoon (March to May), Monsoon (June to September) and retreating monsoon (October to November) periods are 576.1 mm, 1416.4 mm and 99.4 mm respectively. It indicates the need of assured irrigation especially in the winter months and to some extent in the pre-monsoon and retreating monsoon periods. Irrigation is required even in the monsoon period (May to September) because of the erratic nature of the rainfall.

Irrigation in the district started as early as in 1958. In 1971, 6.12 per cent of the total net sown area was irrigated which increased to 14.16 in 1991. In 1991, 83.50 per cent of the total irrigated areas were supplied with water by canals, whereas irrigation done by lift irrigation, deep tubewells and shallow tube wells covered 12.62 per cent and others provided 3.83 per cent of the total irrigated area.

The Dhansiri Irrigation Project irrigates about 5,500 hectares of cultivable land. Table 5.1 and Fig. 5.2 shows the crop-wise irrigated area by Jia Dhansiri Irrigation Project.

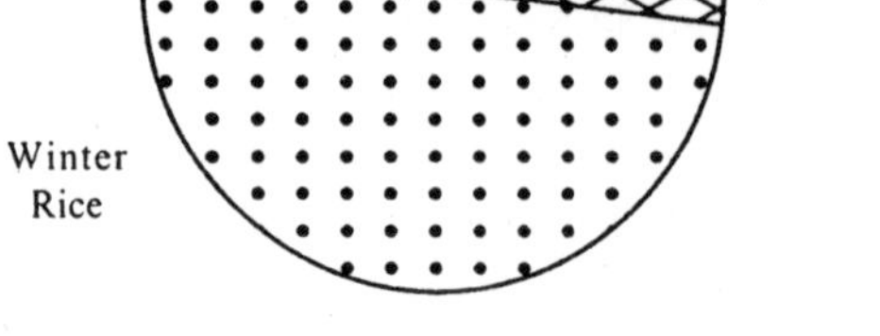

Source : Irrigation Department.

Fig. 5.2 : Cropwise Irrigated Area by Jia-Dhansiri Irrigation Project

Table 5.1 : Crop-wise Irrigated Area (Hectares) by Jia-Dhansiri Irrigation Project

Crops	*Summer rice*	*Winter rice*	*Others*	*Total*
Irrigated area in hectares	2,000	3,000	500	5,500

Source : Office of the Superintending Engineer, Irrigation Department, Darrang.

Out of the total geographical area of 3,18,105 hectares in the Darrang district, 45.17 and 52.72 per cent were devoted to agriculture in 1971 and 1991 respectively as net sown area. The Darrang district produces a variety of crops, such as food crops, oil seeds, vegetables, spices, root crops, fruits etc. Food crop consists of cereals, like paddy, wheat and maize. Among the fibre crops jute is important. Yield per hectare has increased in those areas where irrigation, high yielding variety of seeds and fertilizers are applied.

Development of Agriculture

The pattern of land use reflects the level of agricultural development. Irrigation projects play vital role in selection of crops to be sown, cropping pattern, intensity of cropping, crop combination and use of high yielding variety of seeds and chemical fertilizers in the agricultural field of the district. The irrigation project of Dhansiri influences Udalguri and some parts of Majbat Development Block. These two blocks are considered as areas of high and medium agricultural productivity from the point of view of rank co-efficient of agricultural produce. The net sown area accounts for 80.5 and 69.00 per cent of the total area of Majbot and Udalguri development block respectively. The per hectare yield of almost all the crops under consideration is relatively high in these blocks.

The intensity of cropping is increasing day by day due to increasing pressure of population and use of increasing irrigation. The intensity of cropping is high in this region i.e. 169.33 per cent in immigrant Muslim belt of Majbat and Dalgaon

Sialmari block and 143 per cent in Udalguri block. Double cropping is the common feature of this part of the district. But in some regions where irrigation is practised, three crops a year are grown. The productivity of both summer rice (*Ahu*) and winter rice (*Sali*) are high. Wheat, pulses, rape and mustard, jute, potato, chilli, brinjal, cabbages and cauliflowers, ridge gourd, other crops and vegetables are grown abundantly and their productivity is also high.

The average turnout of major crops has increased in the district since 1961. Table 5.2 shows the average turnout of major crops in Darrang district since 1861 (Fig. 5.3).

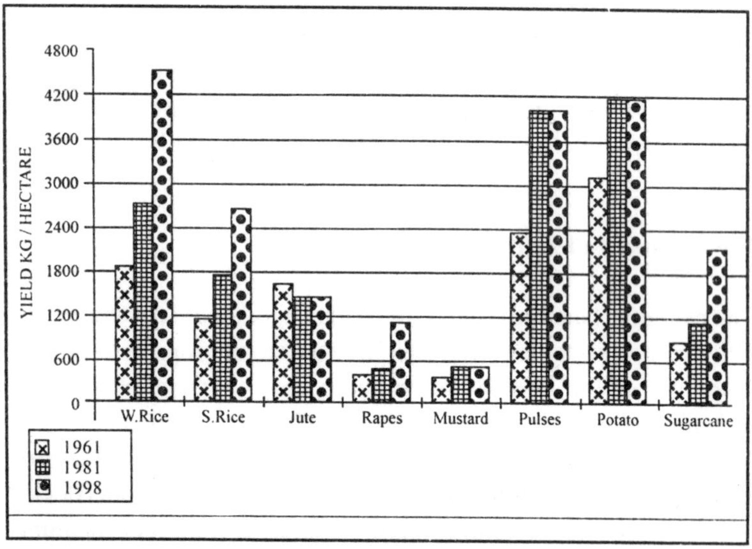

Fig. 5.3 : Average Turnout of Major Crops in Darrang District

For the improvement of agricultural products high yielding variety of seeds have been introduced in Darrang district since 1961. HYV seeds need irrigated water available areas. The area under high yielding variety of seeds increased from 1568 hectares in 1961 to 17230 hectares in 1991 in the district. In 1961, 7213.31 kg. HYV of seeds have been used by Udalguri and Majbat block; but which increase to 30,000 kg. in 1991.

Table 5.2 : Average Turnout of Major Crops in Darrang District since 1961

Crops	*kg/hectare 1961*	*kg/hectare 1981*	*kg/hectare 1998*
Winter rice	1900	2696	5320
Summer rice	1250	1850	2853
Jute	1630	1590	1590
Rape	400	450	1200
Mustard	400	550	550
Pulses	2400	4000	4000
Potato	3200	4200	4200
Sugarcane	1000	1200	2242

Intensity of cropping requires the use of fertilizers, both chemical and organic. The use of high yielding variety of seeds and chemicals fetilizers becomes possible only with assured irrigation. The total area covered by the use of fertilizer in the district was 2245 hectares in 1961, which was increase to 6475 and 16,520 hectares in 1981 and 1991. There is an increase of per hectare consumption of fertilizer in the irrigated areas of Dhansiri irrigation project. The average consumption per hectare of net sown area was 10.13 kg in 1991, as against 2.92 kg in 1988.

As a result of intensification of agriculture and multiple cropping after the diffusion of HYV the traditional rotation of crop has changed. Moreover, the practice of following for the replenishment of soil fertility has also to be given up.

Conclusion

The above description and analysis reveals that the rainfall is erratic and unpredictable in Darrang district, so irrigation is necessary in the region. The Jia-Dhansiri Irrigation project irrigates about 5,500 hectares of culivable land in the district. There has been an increase of net sown area 45.17 per cent to 52.72 per cent of total geographical area. Apart from other factors, greater use of surface canal water is also the factor for increase of intensity of cropping. The average outturn of major crops is increased in the district.

The total area covered by the use of fertilizer in the district is increased. The areas under HYV seeds have also increased. The traditional rotation of crop has changed. The intensity of cropping and agricultural productivity are found to be closely related to use of modern technology like HYV seeds, fertilizers, pesticides, insecticides etc. some problems arise due to irrigation here. The fields are waterlogged due to ignorance of peasants to use irrigated water and soil fertility also decreased.

A scientific land use plan should be prepared and executed with a view to preserve all kinds of forests, grazing lands, charlands etc. and an integrated agricultural development plan should be framed to increase the intensity of cropping by providing adequate inputs. The peasant must be given proper training in agriculture at their own villages with proper demonstration.

REFERENCES

Government of Assam, *Assam District Gazetteer*, Darrang District 1978, Guwahati, Assam.

Government of India, Census Handbook, Darrang District 1951, 1971, 1981, 1991.

Nath, L., Inter Community Variation in Agricultural Land, Occupance in Darrang District. A Geographical Analysis, An unpublished Ph.D. Thesis, Guwahati University.

Saharia Nath, C. (1990), Post Independence Rural Transformation Pattern in Darrang District Assam. An unpublished Ph.D. Thesis, Guwahati University.

Taher and Ahmed (1998), *Geography of North East India : A Comprehensive book for Graduate Course;* published by El-Dorado Publications, Guwahati, 1998.

Taher, M. (1986), Physiographic Framework of North East India, *North Eastern Geographic*, Vol. 18 No. 1 and 2

6

THE GIANT CONFLUENCE ZONE OF LOHIT, DIBANG AND DIHANG
Impact on the Surrounding Regions

BHUBAN GOGOI

The confluence zone of the Lohit, Dibang and the Dihang giving rise to the river Brahmaputra in Upper Assam is the greatest in India and is most unstable in respect of geomorphological pattern and process through time and space. It has great impact on the land and people in the surrounding Jonai Sub-division of the Dhemaji District and Sadiya and Tinsukia Sub-divisions of the Tinsukia district in their mode of peopling, socio-economic development, pattern of human settlement, agricultural practices, etc. The impact is also found to reflect in the perception and responses of the people in the field of their mode of adjustment and fight with the hazards of these rivers. The main hazards of rivers in the region are floods, bank-erosion and channel course shifting, some of which are frequently recurrent and some are continuous. The causes for these lie in the climatic conditions, frequent tectonic acivities and more or less bowl-shaped basin physiography of the region. The major tectonic events of 1897 and 1950 affected the region greatly where the epicenter of the latter lies very near to the region. Parts of the Brahmaputra were subsided down and later soaked with sediments brought down from the surrounding hills and mountains that heavily covered by landslide materials due to the great shocks of the earthquake. As a result, the size of the river got increased, the beds were raised up and heavily braided resulting heavy bank-erosion and channel-shifting. The Dibang was shifted towards east whereas the Dihang was shifted towards west. These events have ultimately resulted in the occurrence of heavy recurrent floods causing great havoc on the one hand and bank-erosion and channel shifting engulfing vast areas that were under human settlement on the other. As the mode of peopling affected, people also developed their mode of resistence and adjustment to these hazards. They adopt both emergency and long-term actions to adjust with these hazards. They develop many flood-proofing systems, rescheduling of crop-calender, practice of agriculture according to physiography, etc. They try to check bank-erosion and divert the shifting channels with their indigenous techniques and limited resource and power. Governments construct few embankments which are not sufficient for the region. No anti-erosion or channel diversion projects were implemented in the region. Embankments, anti-erosion works, channel diversion schemes, construction of dams and reservoirs in mountains are the most urgent works in the region to save it and its people from recurrent disasters.

River basins form natural geomorphological units that not only display the organised relationships among their constituent parameters of land form but the complex interactions of these geomorphological unit with the drainage basins becoming continuously the nucleus points of human civilizations throughout historic and pre-historic times. Man is not only influenced by the river basin where he occurs, but also affects behaviours of the drainage processes (Cooke and Doornkamp, 1974). Man moulds himself while going on moulding the river both socially and individually for building-up of a better life — sustaining environment and socio-economic development. It is in this backdrop in recent times there is an ardent need to develop the river basin on the basis of perfect assessment of the physical situations and the interaction between man and river.

About both the river basin and the interaction between man and river have been widely studied by many in recent years throughout the world in general and western universities in particular. Interactions between man and river in respect of hazards like floods are well-studied and published by many viz. Hoyt and Langbein (1955), Leopold and Maddock (1954), Chow (1964), Chorley (1969), Coates (1974), Unviersity of Chicago Department of Geography [research papers by White, 1945, 1961, 1964; White *et al.* 1958; Murphy, 1958; Sheaffer, 1960; Kates, 1962, 1965; Sewell, 1965; UNESCO (1969), etc. River basin environment study is widely done worth of which to be mentioned are the works of Leopold, Wolman and Miller (1964), Chorley (1969), Coates (1971), Gregory (1977) etc.]. These works have laid down the firm foundations and complete methodology for the study of the impact of rivers on man and human response to it. In the light of the essence of these studies, here efforts have been made to search the impact of the confluence of the three rivers, viz. Lohit, Dibang and Dihang of the Brahmaputra on man and the mode of human responses to them in turn. Due to dearth of necessary data, only suitable methods are used with certain limitations here. Large scale maps of different times, recent satellite imagery and field experiences are used for finding out the channel changes, dimensions of the river regime, etc. Data from both the primary and secondary sources are used to understand the situations. Efforts also have been made to find out solutions to adverse situations and recommended at the end of the study.

The confluence zone of the Lohit, Dibang and the Dihang (Fig. 6.1) giving rise to the river Brahmaputra in Upper Assam of N.E. India that located at around 95°30′ E and 27°45′ N is the greatest in India in respect of extension, water discharge and sediment yield. The river Brahmaputra has been geomorphologically remained unstable and qualitatively under the process of metamorphosis since 1950 great earthquake. The confluence zone being its part has been opening an another chapter of hazardous impact on the land and people of the region surrounding and at distant of it. The dreadful folds, the regular bankline change, the shifting of channels etc. bring threat to and uncertainity of life and constrict the socio-economic development in the region, whereas the river was and still in many quarters is a blessing to the people of N.E. India in general.

Physical Environment

The zone of the confluence is occurred by three gigantic rivers as mentioned above that are equally gigantic with size of the mighty Brahmaputra at the head of the Brahmaputra valley. The catchment areas of the Dihang, Dibang and the Lohit are 2,45,000 km^2, 12,120 km^2 and 22,077 km^2 respectively that conversely form a bowl-shaped basin with the only opening toward west with more or less steep slopes from surrounding hills to plains. Fifty per cent of the catchment area by the Lohit and only 6 per cent of the catchment area of the Dihang fall within India. The Dibang river catchment area falls completely with India. The valley head of the Brahmaputra comprises not only the confluencing river channels but also flat active flood lain extended broadly towards both bank interspersed by large number of spill channels and tributaries which do facilitate the easy spill of flood waters and shifting of channels during flood seasons.

Table 6.1 : Major River Confluences in India Total and Average Discharge of Water

Confluences	*Totally yearly discharge in million cu. m.*	*Average Discharge in cumecs*
1. Indus-Sutlej-Kuram	1,97,365	6,258.4
2. Ganga-Yamuna	1,52,000	4,819.9
3. Lohit-Dibang-Dihang	3,22,800	10,235.9

Source : Rao, K. L. (1979) *India's Water Wealth*, Orient Longman Ltd., New Delhi.

The confluence zone of the Lohit, Dibang and the Dihang carry largest volume of water (Table 6.1) in India. The confluencing rivers supply 22 per cent of the total water discharge measured at the outlet of the Brahamaputra from Assam Valley (Rao, 1979). Again the amount of water discharge varies from time to time throughout the basin. The flood of 1962 had a water discharge of 73,100 cumecs measured at Pandu, Guwahati of whose 46 per cent of the water was contributed by the Dihang alone.

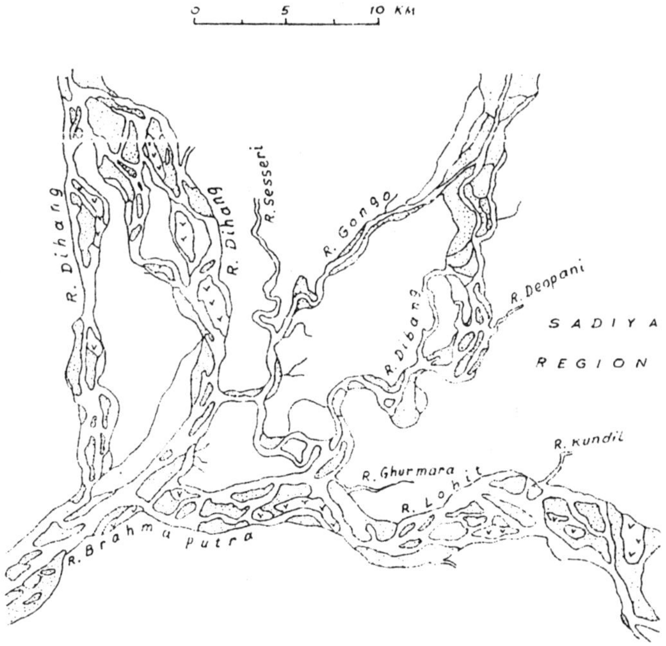

Fig. 6.1 : The Confluence and its adjacent Areas Islands and Sandbars of Rivers, 1913-14

The confluencing rivers have fairly braided channels with islands and sand bars in their midst (Fig. 6.2). Some delta shaped islands are built up at the mouth of these rivers in this zone. The reason for development of these delta shaped islands is perhaps due to both the estuarine effect of the large confluencing water masses acting as a local base level of erosion and the branching effect of the channels. The Lohit is also going to form this type of island at its mouth. The braiding indices increase from 3.4 to 3.82 on average during 1913-73 in all these rivers. The channel courses are fringed by a low flood-wash or active flood-plain zone which is full of flood spill channels. Turbulent flood rushing down from the surrounding hills regularly come across this plain inundating thousands of heactares of land of Jonai and Dhemaji sub-divisions of the Dhemaji district and Sadiya and Tinsukia sub-divisions of Tinsukia district. The combined water of these rivers has to face constriction to enter

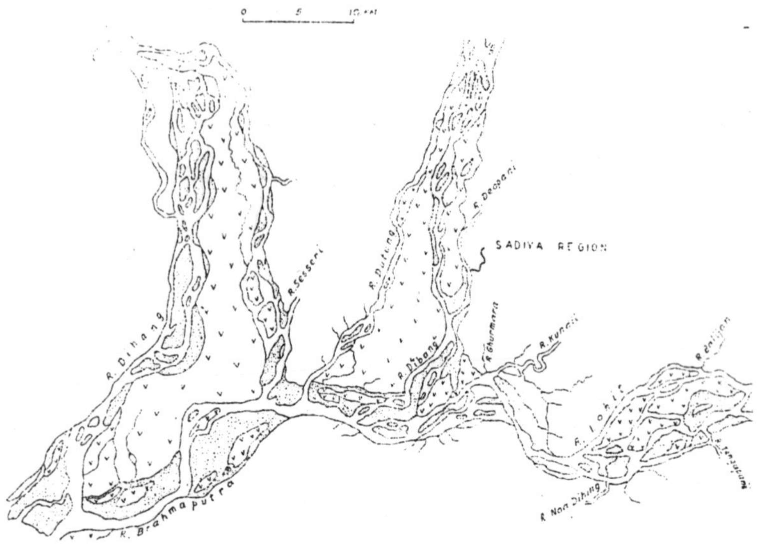

Fig. 6.2 : The Confluence and Adjacent Areas Islands and Sandbars of River Beds, 1973-74

into the single channel of the Brahmaputra and become slightly steep at this length. Therefore, floods, bank-erosion and channel shifting are common in this region. Again more frequently these hazards are found to occur in association with tectonic activities in the past especially before 1966 (Gogoi and Barman, 1991). The great earthquakes of 1897 and 1950 had tremendous effect on the pattern and process of the rivers in the region. These two earthquakes, especially the latter changed the geomorphology of old order and brought the river Brahmaputra under spectacular process of metamerphosis. The sub-mergence, siltation and expansion were the immediate effects of the earthquake. Due to deposition of landslide debris on beds, the rivers become wider, shallower and steeper resulting in the building up of braids and new channels in the region.

Though climatic variability in respect of rainfall amount and number of rainy days, are exhibiting a decreasing trend, the water discharge of the river are found significantly increasing (Table 6.2). This is perhaps due to the destruction of forest, more integration of drainage systems, soil erosion, clearance of drainage channels, etc.

Table 6.2 : The Lohit, Dibang and the Dihang Pattern of Water Discharge in cumecs

Rivers	*Water discharge in cumecs*		
	1932	*1958-66*	*1979**
Lohit	958	1478	4903
Dibang	771	1240	1991
Dihang	1572	5866	6342

* These data were published in 1979, but the recording year is not known.
Source : Burrard and Hayen (1932), CWC (1958-66) and RQQ (1979).

The rate of sedimentation had not monitored in the past, not even in the present times too. The extent of sedimentation may be traced and mentioned from many studies. The Brahmaputra and the Dibang were subsided down and silted upto 3 m and 6 m respectively in this zone by the great earthquake of 1950 (National Flood Commission, 1980). Again the 1100 km long navigable waterway extended from the mouth of the Brahmaputra upto beyond Sadiya had to be suspended after 1962 due to heavy siltation on river-beds. The siltation reached the height of the roof of the railway station building at Saikhowa immediately after 1950 great earthquake. Increase of braiding in the rivers is already mentioned before. Ofcourse, a study in the recent sedimentary budget (1971-79) shows a decreasing trend of sedimentation due to excess out-flow of sediments from the rivers of this zone surpassing the rate of sedimentation. But during 1957-71 period, it shows an increasing rate of sedimentation on the beds of the rivers in this zone (Goswami, 1985). During the period of 1971-79, excess out flow of sediments through suspended load does not necessarily mean the decreasing rate of sedimentation, but it means the clearance of the channels or erosion on the banklines extending the length of channel cross-sections in this area. Thus these rivers become many times wider than the older ones.

The effect of these changing situation ultimately were the occurrence of hazards of floods, bank-erosion and channel shifting which are briefly outlined below:

The Flood

The surrounding region of the confluence is a playground of regularly recurrent floods. The active floodplain zones being full of spill-channels are tremendously affected. The Dibru-Saikhowa Reserve Forest in the south is a parennial floodprone area. The water of this area during the flood of 1993 rose upto 137.6 m at the Ananta Nalla. The flood depth varies from 2 m to 6 m. Floods breach the existing embankments both in the north and the south.

Bankline Shift and Bank Erosion

The shifting of bankline associated with bank erosion is a continuous process of the channel though more intensive during flood times. It is noticed that the width of the Brahmaputra between banks increase for more than 4 times in general and more than 6 times in particular during the period of 1913-84. The Dibang retreats for as much as 5 km and advances for more than 8 km on its left from its old banks of 1913. The Lohit advances for 7 km at maximum towards north and 5 km at maximum towards south on its right and left banklines respectively with sufficient amount of retreations from its old banks of 1913. The Dibang advances from 7 km and retreats for 4 km at maximum on its right bank. The left bank has also sufficient extent of advancement and retreation during this period (1913-84). Again periodic shifting during this period often cross the mentioned levels. These shifting of banks are associated with both the dangerous bank erosion and channel shifting and dreadful destruction of life and property in the region.

Channel Course Shifting

River channel course shifting is more conspicuous in this region. Enlargement and bank erosion of the rivers are largely found to occur through active shifting of channels and later merging them with the main rivers. The shifting of channels occurs through off-shooting distributaries or anabranching of channels or shortening the meanders all due to excess force and water volume of the river.

The shifting is also occurred through the caputre of the lower parts of the tributaries that run for some distance parallel to the main streams and meet them by forming acute angles. Due to shifting of the main rivers, the old concentric confluence is now bifurcated and departed. The Dihang and the Dibang have shifted themselves mutually from each other towards the west and the east respectively. The Dibang now uses to flow through the lower course of the Ghurmara river. The Dibang previously captured the lower course of the Deopani river. The Lohit also now uses to flow through the Ananta Nalla towards south of the Lohit-Brahmaputra alignment to empty into the Dibru river. In this way, quite a large number of lower courses of tributaries like Kundil, Ghurmara, Dikrong, Deopani, Saikhowa, Ghilani, Balijan, Tengapani, etc. were captured by the major rivers in the region. In this way, expansion and retreation, bank erosion and depositions are continuously occurring more conspicuously within this region than other through channel course shifting.

Impact of Rivers on the People

Despite the fact that the rivers have their dreadful hazards which often become the only cause of destruction of human civilization, the river valley yet becomes the major life sustaining habitat of human being. This mystery is also used to occur in this region. Impact of rivers by their suitability or adversity makes man experience to develop his own capacity to manage the situations. To develop the conditions more by fully utilizing the prospects, the people fight with the adverses or adjust with the possible by adopting many techniques from time to time. Some of these impact and human responses that observed in this region are discussed in the following.

Impact on Population and Settlement

Due to riverine geomorphological situations, low population pressure, presence of deep jungles and occurrence of ethnic troubles, the process of peopling in this region was under the phases of ebbs and tides in the past. People used to settle on higher and better grounds e.g. the levees devoid of flood menace in the past, but the great tectonic activities of 1950 aggrevated the situation. Due to decrease of the tectonic activities from the later part of the seventies, increase of population pressure and pacification of ethnic troubles after Independence, the population is slowly increasing but not upto the mark (Table 6.3). Table 6.3 shows the densities of population of the administrative units which include the flood free high areas including the urban centres esepcially in case of the Tinsukia Sub-division. Therefore it will not give the proper picture of the active flood plain zone, but may project the level of least population densities expectedly far below the state level. 67 per cent of the population of Jonai Sub-division and also consierable portion of the Sadiya and Tinsukia Sub-divisions in this area are composed of tribals, specially the Mishings and Deoris.

The old human settlements were concentrated along the river banks (water point or levees) or around the agricultural fields where the intensity or depth of flood was less or was no flood. Today people use to live along the road sides which can facilitate them for better communication, emergency evacuations or temporary settlement on roads due to flood.

Table 6.3 : The Lohit, Dibang and the Dihang Population Densities of Neighbourhood Administrative Units

Sub-divisions / State	*Population Density, Person per km²*	
	1971	*1991*
1. Jonai	29	104
2. Sadiya	60	98
3. Tinsukia	225*	237
Assam	186	286

* including the present Margherita Sub-division.
Source : Stastical Handbook 1971 and 1991.

House types are both of bamboo made or wooden platform type used by the tribals and high earthen plinth type used and suitable for flood proofing. People are found displaced in large numbers annually due to flood, bank erosion and deposition and channel shifting.

Agriculture, Land-use and Socio-economic Conditions

Agriculture, especially the rice, is done by rescheduling the time adjusting with the occurrence of flood. Often relatively high lands are brought under cultivation. At low lying marshy areas winter rice ('Baw' rice) is practised. Crop failure or loss is a common scence in this region when the flood frequency and intensity are high and duration is long. Agriculture is damaged by long-stagnant flood water or by silt and sand deposits or erosion by flood currents and shifting of channels. Rabi crops are generally practised in the flood affected areas during off time (winter). Vegetables and other horticultural crops are produced largely during winter season. Animal rearing both for milk and meat are practised in the grasslands of chars, river islands, sandy bank areas, high lands or relatively safe areas are used for settlement, tea-cultivation, etc. The total net sown area varies from time-to-time depending on the intensity of flood.

Human Perception and Responses

A deemed uncertanity prevails in the perception of the people to hazards in the region. People become frustrated when alternative ways are limited. They have forgotten the otherwise normal life in the region and try to fight or adjust with hazards. They use to fight with hazards through the development of flood proofing houses with scaffolding or high plinth type, constructing platforms both inside or outside their houses or other traditional of indigenous techniques. They construct dams to divert small channels flood currents, plant trees on river banks, agricultural fields and bastiland to check flood currents and erosion and construct highlands for safety. They do adjust with these hazards by rescheduling their crop calendar, rescheduling their crop practice using conventions of physiography, etc. They develop their own warning system and method of emergency evacuations. They take shelter temporarily at higher places like roads, high mounds at flood times. They use country boat, 'bhur' (made of body of banana trees) for emergency evacuations. They are generally well swimers and use this art for their rescue and other works. But when these all efforts fail, they use to migrate elsewhere or suffer from loss. The Government constructs embankments on the south bank of the Lohit at Saikhowa side and on the north bank of the Brahmaputra in the Dhemaji district, but these are not well maintained and repaired and nor sufficient to cheek the menace of flood. The Government also constructs ring bunds, and implements drainage works, land development projects, afforestation projects, etc. It also supplies emergency relief and rescue operations, after flood help and assistance to the people. But there works are very much insufficient or people have to suffer frequently without help from any sources. The flood protection works are not only insufficient but also not upto the mark and the flood waters generally breach up or wash away them easily. Anti-erosion spurs and channel diversion dams are practically not present in this region. Therefore the region becomes a playground of flood, bank erosion and channel shifting not only in the active floodplain zone, but also very often destruct heavily the normal flood free area bringing great threat to the whole region.

Conclusions and Recommendations

From this study, it is found that the rivers of the confluence zone have tremendous affects on land and people of its surrounding region. Floods and bank erosion are found all over Assam along the Brahmaputra, but channel shifting is particularly and conspicuously found only within this region. Tectonic activity modifies the geomorphological processes within the region which influence the mode of peopling and socio-economic development of the region. People live in this region through development of adjustment techniques, fighting with or suffering loss to gemorphological hazards of the river. The urgent tasks here to solve the problem are outlined below :

1. The region is to be studied thoroughly basing on long-term monitored data to find out the geomorphological processes and patterns.
2. The impact of these processes and patterns on man is also to be studied to develop the intreractions between man and nature.

3. Embankments, anti-erosion spurs, river training or channel diversion spurs and dams are to be constructed to alleviate the problems. The existing works are to be revitalised and repaired urgently.
4. For the permanent solution of the problems, the proposed construction of dams on the Dihang, Dibang and the Lohit in the mountainous area is to be completed as early as possible which will not only effect the micro region, but North East India as a whole.
5. People are to be encouraged and trained to develop their mode of adjustment and fights with hazards. Relief and economic assistance should be given, rehabilitation, crop and property insurance are to be done urgently and effectively without fail. The infrastructure for development need to be developed for better life in the micro region.

REFERENCES

Chorley, R. J. (ed.) (1969), *Water, Earth and Man,* Mathuen London.

Chow, V.T. (ed.) (1964), *Handbook of Applied Hydrology,* McGraw Hill, New York.

Coates, D.R. (1971), *Environmental Geomorphology,* State University of New York, Binghamton.

Coates, D.R. (1971), *Environmental Geomorphology and Landscape Conservation* Vol. I, II & III Hutehinson and Ross Inc., Pensylvania.

Cooke R.U. and J.C. Doorkamp, (1974), *Geomorphology in Environmental Management — An Introduction,* Clarendon Press, Oxford, London.

Gogoi, B. and R. Barman (1991), The Course of the Buri-Dihing River — A Study in Historical Geomorphology, *North-Eastern Geographer,* Vol. 23 No. 1&2.

Goswami, D.C. (1985), Brahmaputra River, Assam, India, Physiography, Basin Denudation and Channel Aggradation, *Water Resource Research,* Vol. 21 No. 7 pp. 959-978.

Gregory, K.J. (1977), River Channel Changes, John Wiley and Sons Ltd.

Hoyt, W.A. and W.B. Langbein, (1955), *Floods,* Ronald Press, New York.

Kates, R.W. (1962), *Hazard and Choice Perception in Floodplain Management,* University of Chicago, Department of Geography Research Paper 78.

Kates, R.W., (1965), *Industrial Flood Losses,* University of Chicago, Dept. of Geography Research Paper 98.

Leopold, L.B., M.G. Wolman and J.P. Miller (1964), *Fluvial Processes in Geomorphology,* Eurasia Publishing House (Pvt.) Ltd., New Delhi.

7

STREAMS OF SHILLONG
An Ecological Overview

ABHIK GUPTA

INTRODUCTION

The civil station of Shillong was established in 1864 as the administrative centre for a Khasi and Jaintia Hills district. At that time most of its present area was covered with deep forests with Laban — a small village under the United Khasi State of Shillong — nestling on the hill slopes. On March 20, 1874, Shillong was declared the capital of then Assam Province and remained as the administrative capital of the entire North Eastern Region for a long time. Thus the existence of Shillong as an administrative centre as well as a hill resort for over 100 years, and eventually the creation of the State Meghalaya in 1972, whose capital it became, provided tremendous incentives for urban growth and proliferation. However, like most of its counterparts in the country, the growth and proliferation of Shillong has been largely haphazard and unplanned. Besides creating a score of other environmental problems such as deforestation, overcrowding, traffic congestion, slum formation, air pollution and the like. This growth has severely affected the environmental status of the streams that drain the Greater Shillong area. This is manifested, among other aspects, in their altered and often defused physical conditions, degraded water quality and declining biodiversity. The present review trace the broad patterns that emerge from the information available on the physical, chemical and biological aspects of these streams along with the anthropogenetic activities responsible for their degradation and pollution (Gupta, 1980, 1984, 1992, 1994, 1995, 1996; Gupta and Michael, 1992; Ao *et al.* 1984; Nath and Gupta 1993; Husain, 1984).

The Study Area

Geography, Geology and Climate

Shillong lies on the deeply dissected Meghalaya Plateau which runs in an East-West direction. The greater Shillong area is bound by the co-ordinates of 25°32′10″ to 25° 36′20″N latitude and 91°51′ 30″ to 91°56′30″E longitude. The uppermost part of this area is a mildly undulating plateau top with an altitude of 1900 m as *l*, the highest points being the Shillong peak (1964 m) and the Laitkor Peak (19600 m). Below this lies the Shillong basin with an altitude of c 15m with several flat low relief (maximum 80 m) hillocks with gently undulating valley as well as moderate relief hills having escarpments on two sides in mesa or butte formation (G.S.I., unpubl.). Land forms are mostly erosional, although depositional land forms with recent alluvium are present in the floodplains of Umkhrah stream in the Polo Valley.

The rocks in this area are mostly pre-cambrian quartzites either exposed or covered with thin layers of laterite, subordinate phyllites and slates are present in certain places. These rocks are often intruded by epi-dioritic rocks known as "Khasi greenstones" (G.S.I. unpubl.). Shillong has a subtropical mountain climate with annual rainfall ranging from 2000-2500 mm with mean annual temperature between 16-17°C (Husain, 1984).

Running Water Systems

The Shillong valley is drained by numerous small streams which originate on the northern slope of the Laitkor range of hills from groundwater sources. These in turn join to form two main stream system — Umkhrah and Umshirpi — which ultimately from the Beadon and Bishop Waterfalls respectively. Below the fall their combined flow known as Wah Ro Ro eventually joins the Umiam river which is one of the major rivers draining the northern slope of the Meghalaya Pleateau. Another major stream, Umsing, skirts of the city of Shillong, flowing beyond Mawlai area. Before, the impoundment of river Umiam for hydel power generation, this stream used to flow into the former, but presently it flows along the old course of river Umiam below the reservoir.

Based on the land use pattern in the catchment areas of the streams, four longitudinal zones could be identified. Zone A comprises dense forest of the Riat Laban Reserve, through which some of the headwater streams of Umshirpi system such as, Wah Diengling, Wah Risa, Wah Crinoline and Wah Moti Nagar flow. In this zone, the stream valleys have retained an intact and mixed riverine forest comprising several trees and shurbs such as *Pinus Kesiya, Quercus* spp., *Acacia* spp., *Rhododendron* spp. etc. Zone B comprises those sections of the streams where they flow through degraded forests, almost exclusively composed of *Pinus Kesiya*. Zone C is in areas dominated by waste pastures, cultivated plots and light urban build-up, while Zone D includes urban areas in the catchment of both Umkhrah and Umshirpi.

Ecology of the Stream

Water Quality

Several studies have investigated the water quality of Shillong streams based on selected physico-chemical variables in their water. Of these, two earlier studies (Gupta, 1980; Ao *et. al.*, 1984) were carried out during 1976-78, while the others (Nath and Gupta, 1993; Gupta, 1994, 1996) present the data recorded during 1990-1992. Thus, these studies allow us to compare the physico-chemical status of the streams within a 15 year time span or so. Table 7.1 summarises these comparisons. However, a total comparison is not possible as neither the sites nor the parameters examined tally completely.

Furthermore, data on heavy metal concentrations and bacteriological parameters are not available for the 1976-1978 periods.

Table 7.1 : Water Quality in Streams of Shillong during 1976-1992

Parameters	*Period*	*Zones*			
		A	*B*	*C*	*D*
pH	1	—	6.9-7.3	6.4-6.8	7.2-7.3
	2	6.1-6.3	6.1-6.3	6.5-7.1	6.4-7.2
Conductivity μScm^{-1}	1				
	2	12.7-15	23.1-46.2	31.9-57.8	105-183
Dissolved Oxygen mgl^{-1}	1	—	8.1-8.4	6.4-8.7	6.0-6.3
Total alkalinity mgl^{-1}	1	—	23-26	10-18	34-49
	2	14-20	20-26	31-44	44-100.8
Chloride mgl^{-1}	2	9-12	11-16	11-23	25-31.5
Hardness mgl^{-1}	2	7-8	12-16	16-32	24-56
Total solids mgl^{-1}	2	34-36	36-43	43-53	58-265
Nitrate $Nmgl^{-1}$	1	—	0.1-0.16	0.18-0.21	0.64-0.72
	2	Tr.-0.1	0.06-0.28	0.33-1.85	2.68-8.0
B.O.D. mgl^{-1}	2	ND	ND	0.3	30.5-45.7
C.O.D. mgl^{-1}	2	ND	ND	40	147.8-162.0
Total Coliform (MPN/100 ml)	2	—	—	430	9000-160000
Faecal Coliform (MPH/100ml)	2	—	—	0	2600-35000
Cadmium μgl^{-1}	2	<0.5	—	4.5 ± 4.0	—
Copper μgl^{-1}	2	<1.0	—	25.4 ± 9.2	—
Manganese μgl^{-1}	—	<1.0	—	204.5 ± 84.6	—
Lead μgl^{-1}	2	<10.0	0	27.3 ± 14.0	—
Zinc μgl^{-1}	2	4.3	—	37.6 ± 25.3	—

Period 1 : 1976-1978; *Period 2 :* 1990-1992; *Tr. : Trace;* ND : Below detection limit.

Sources : Gupta, 1980, 1994, 1996; Ao *et al.*, 1984; Nath and Gupta, 1993.

Nevertheless, it is evident from Table 7.1 that if the water quality parameters are compared on a temporal scale, appreciable deterioration in water quality could be seen to have occurred in Zone D, and to some extent in Zone C, while Zone D, and to some extent in Zone C, while Zone A and B have remained largely unaltered. For instance, the nitrate concentration in Zones C and D have increased about 1.8-8.8 and 4.2-11.1 times respectively, while total alkalinity has more than doubled in some Zone D sites. In contrast, there is a marked reduction in dissolved oxygen in certain Zone D sites like Polo and Mawlai.

When water quality in the different zones are compared a clear longitudinal zonation with progressive deterioration as the streams leave the protected forest area to first enter degraded forests, then waste pastures and cultivated areas, and finally areas with dense urban build up (Table 7.1). Also, these longitudinal differences are more marked, during 1990-92 than during 1976-78, indicating accentuated environmental degradation in the downtown areas during the latter period. Several variables such as conductivity, total alkalinity, chloride, hardness, total solids, nitrate, B.O.D. and C.O.D. register sharp increase in Zone D, as compared to the other zones. Dissolved oxygen, in contrast, declines rapidly. The bacterial contamination is also very high in Zone D sites on Umkhrah and Umshirpi. Furthermore, concentrations of heavy metals record a sharp rise from near undetectable levels in Zone A to fairly high values in Zone C. All these evidences, therefore, point towards the adverse impact of urban growth in Shillong on the water quality of its streams. However, the presence of the Riat Laban Forest Reserve along the headwater of stream has contributed towards preservation of water quality in Zone A and a large extent in Zone B, as revealed by data presented in Table 7.1.

Biodiversity in Streams

Gupta (1992) reported the presence of 35 morphospecies of benthic aquatic insects in the streams of Shillong region, excluding those found in River Umiam. However, later studies have added another 5 morphospecies to this list, bringing it to 40. Of other, around 17 are confined to River Umsing in those are where it flows through deep gorges below Mawlai (Gupta, 1980). Of the others, permanent populations of about 6 taxa are found only in Zone A, where the streams flow through dense, mixed forest. In the event of any further denudation of vegetation in the currently protected areas, these sensitive taxa are likely to become endangered.

Table 7.2 : Ranges of Diversity/Biotic Index Values in Different Zones of Shillong Streams based on Benthic Macroinvertebrate Diversity.

Diversity/Block Index	*Zones*			
	A	*B*	*C*	*D*
Species - Richness (S)	15-20.5	10.5-14.5	7-10	3-9
Spannon-Wiener (H')	3.43-4.08	2.45-3.03	1.85-2.81	1.02-29
Margalef (d')	3.42-5.3	2.23-3.26	1.44-2.01	0.32-1.85
Chandler (%) ASPT	68.7-71.2	61.6-67.7	47.6-53.5	34.750.7
BMWP-ASPT	6.28-6.67	5.71-6.62	3.66-4.63	2.67-4.11

Source : Gupta, 1994.

Sensitive Taxa in Shillong Streams :

1. Diatoms (Periphytonic); Gomphonema, Tabellaria, Navicula, Synedra etc.
2. Invertebrates : Crabs, Case-building caddisflies, Heptageniidae, *Leptophlebiidae* (Mayflies), *Plecoptera* (Stoneflies).
3. Fish : *Garra gotyla, G. lyssorhynchus, Accrossocheilus hexagonolepis.*

Gupta (1994) determined several diversity and biotic indices for streams based on their benthic macro invertebrate diversity. As shown in Table 7.2, all the index values show sharp decline from Zone A to Zone D. Thus anthropogenetic activities in Shillong area have inflicted major damages on the biodiversity in streams. Besides, the invertebrates, several species of fishes like *Garra lyssorhynchus, G. gotyla* and *Accrossocheilus hexagonolepis* have also become rare in the streams (Gupta, 1992). Crabes are also found now in the forested headwater reaches only.

Nature of Anthropogenic Distrubances

Deforestation

Extensive forestation in the catchments of the streams has taken place during the last few decades, reducing the forest cover in Greater Shillong area from about 3940.76 ha to a mere 1220 ha (Nath and Gupta, 1993). Several factors like agricultural activities including 'bun' method of cultivation on hill slopes, timberlogging, quarrying, road construction and urban proliferation are responsible for decimation of forest cover in this area. The floristic composition has also changed from a mixed forest characterized by *Pinus Kesiya, Quercus dealbzata, Q. griffithi, Schima khasiana* and *Acacia* sp. To degraded forests dominated by P. kesiya (Nath and Gupta, 1993). It is known that removal of riparian vegetation eliminates sensitive species by altering the light-shade and temperature regimes, and resulting in shortage of suitable food when mixed forests are replaced by monocultures such as that of pine (Woodall and Wallace, 1972; Newbold *et al.*, 1980; Resh and Rosenberg, 1984).

Stone and Sand Quarrying

More than 15 stone/sand quarries are operating in this area, some of which are located near streams. The fine quartzite sand from the quarries are deposited into the streams via surface run off and aerial deposition.

Agricultural Activities

The 'bun' method of potato cultivation is prevalent, besides some permanent cultivation in stream valley. The rate of soil erosion from exposed slopes, quarries and cultivated plots is estimated to be around 40-50 tonnes/ha/yr (Prasad *et al.*, 1981).

Stone/sand Collection from Streambed

This practice result in gross alteration of streambed structure and reduction of substratum heterogeneity, which in turn, are known to reduce diversity of periphytonic algae, invertebrates and fishes (Resh and Rosenberg, 1984; Gupta and Michael, 1992).

Urban Development

The population in Shillong Urban Area in 1991 was 2,22,273 with a growth rate of 42.3 per cent during 1971-81 and 27.2 per cent during 1981-91 (Sharma, 1995). To meet the increasing demand for housing, slums have emerged in parts of Police Bazar, Ewduh, Garikhana, Polo Bazar-Nongmynsong-Pynthorumkhrah and other areas. Some of these slums have cope up near streams, often encroaching part of the streambed. The sewage and sullage, as well as a large part of solid wastes, both from the slums and from the other parts of the city are deposited into the streams. It is estimated that even if only 10 per cent of the total solid waste load of 150,000 tonnes/yr. is deposited into the streams, it would amount to about 15,000 tonnes/yr. Much of these wastes are finally deposited into the Umiam Reservoir via Wah Ro Ro and River Umiam. All these practices have resulted in congestion of flow and deterioration of water quality, inspite of which, the stream water is still used for bathing and washing, especially by the economically weaker sections.

Conclusion and Recommendations

In spite of being mostly first and second order streams of relatively small size and low discharge, the running water systems of Shillong are ecologically important as they originate from the northern slope of the Laitkor range that represents the highest part of the Meghalaya Plateau and is an important water divide. It is, therefore, important to study the biodiversity in these systems. Furthermore, after the creation of the Umiam Reservoir, the run off from the entire Shillong basin is transported to the reservoir via these systems. As the studies cited in this review reveal, increased sediment load and sewage contamination, Shillong streams are not only affecting their own water quality and biodiversity, but also that in the Umiam Reserviour. Consequently, not only important fish species such as the Chocolate Mahseer (*Accrossocheilus hexagonolepis)* resident in the reservoir is being threatened, the tourism prospects may also be adversely affected due to pollution and the resultant growth of fouling organisms like blue-green algae and various dipterans, oligochaetes and others.

The studies also show the importance of the Riat Laban Forest Reserve in maintenance of water quality and conservation of biodiversity. The presence of this protected area has ensured that the headwater zones of the streams have remained largely unaltered during the last 15 years. However, to prevent any further deterioration of stream water quality and ecology in the urban area, and to improve the situation, the following measures may be adopted:

(i) entry of untreated sewage into the streams must be stopped;
(ii) the stream banks should be cleared, as far as possible, of slums or any other encroachments;
(iii) wherever possible, buffer strips comprising a belt of riparian vegetation several metres wide should be created on the stream banks;
(iv) quarrying near streams as well as indiscriminate collection of stone/sand from streambeds must be totally prohibited; and
(v) a general awareness about the need to conserve these streams ought to be generated by popularising among the youth the folklores associated with many of these streams or areas nearby, and by emphasizing their ecological and economic importance as well.

REFERENCES

Ao, M., Alfred, J.R.B. and Gupta, A. (1984). Studies on Some Lotic Systems in the North Eastern Hills Region of India, *Limnologica* (Berlin) 15:135-141.

Gupta, A. (1980). "On the Taxonomy and Biology of Ephemeroptera (Mayflies) of Meghalaya State, India" unpublished Ph.D. Thesis, North-Eastern Hills University, Shillong.

Gupta, A. (1984). Observations on Human Interference in some running water systems of Meghalaya. In *Status of Ecology* (Jawal, I.J.S., Ed.), pp. 61-68, Punjab Publishing House, Patiala.

Gupta, A. (1992). Impact of Deforestation on the Aquatic Fauna of Meghalaya. In *Environment Conservation and Wasteland Development in Meghalaya* (Gupta A. and Dhar, D.C., Eds.), pp. 128-139, Meghalaya Science Society, Shillong.

Gupta, A. (1994). A Comparative Assessment of Methods for Biological Surveillance of Running Water Quality using Macroinvertebrates. In *Proc. 3rd Natl. Symp. Environment* (Nair, B. Eapen, C.D., Bapat, V.N., Sadasivan, S. and Gangadharan, P., Eds.) pp. 209-213, Board of Research in Nuclear Sciences, Department of Atomic Energy, Government of India.

Gupta, A. (1995). Impacts of Urbanization on Fresh Water Systems with special reference to North-East India. In *Urbanization and Development in North-East India — Trends and Policy Implications* (Ganguly, J.B. Ed.), pp. 77-81, Deep and Deep Publications, New Delhi.

Gupta, A. (1996). Heavy Metals in Water, Periphytonic Algae, Detritus, and Insects from Two Streams in Shillong, North Eastern India, *Environment Monit. Assess* 40:215-223.

Gupta, A. and Michael, R.G. (1992). "Diversity, Distribution and Seasonal Abundance of Ephemeroptera in Streams of Meghalaya State, India". *Hydrobiologia* 228:131-139.

Hussain, Z. (1984) : Ecological Implications of Environmental Factors in the Meghalaya Plateau Ecosystem. In *Status of Ecology* (Jaswal, I.J.S., Ed.) pp. 69-77, Punjab Publishing House, Patiala.

Nath, H. and Gupta, A. (1993). Status of Environmental Pollution in Shillong (1981-91) — An Overview. In *Dynamics of Tribal Soceity — A Micro-study* (Datta Ray, B. and Agnihotri, S.K. Eds.), pp. 41-64, Uppal Publishing House, New Delhi.

Newbold, J.D., Erman, D.C. and Roby, K.B. (1980). Effects of Logging on Macroinvertebrates in Streams with or without Buffer Strips. *Can.J. Fish. Aquat. Sci.* 37:1076-1085.

Prasad, R.N., Ram, P., Barooah, R.C. and Ram, M. (1981). Soil Fertility Management in NEH Region. *Research Bulletin No. 9.* ICAR Research Complex for NEH Region, Shillong.

Sharma, S. (1995). Urban Growth and its Trend in Meghalaya. In *Urbanization and Development in North-East India — Trends and Policy Implications* (Ganguly, J.B., Ed.) pp. 215-223, Deep and Deep Publications, New Delhi.

Woodall, W.R. and Wallace, J.B. (1972). The Benthic Fauna in Four Small Southern Appalachian Streams. *Amer Midl. Naturalist* 88:393-407.

8

URBANISATION AND THE STREAMS OF SHILLONG

SUBRATA PURKAYASTHA and SUSMITA DAS

Most of Indian towns and cities have often grown in an unplanned way. The growth in most cases has been rapid with almost spontaneous and uncontrolled expansion that has been generated by migration and natural growth. These in trun poses serious environmental problem, which calls for proper environmental planning.

Again each urban area has its unique geomorphology, which may play a significant role in the field of urban landuse especially in the hilly and rugged topographic area.

Shillong being a plateau characterizsed by moderate to steep slope and rugged terrain calls for an understanding the landforms and the fluvial process before any urban planning is undertaken. However, due to the unplanned nature of growth coupled with deforestation in the waxing slope of Shillong for constructional activities have resulted to soil erosion, which in turn has resulted to the siltation in the streams of Shillong. The haphazard development of the urban functions has also resulted to the stream pollution. As more land comes under constructional activities the streams in certain areas have been filled resulting to a total drying up of the streams in certain cases and in some cases there is seepage of water resulting to severe leaching of the soil, the flush action of streams has also been restricted. But before we go into an analysis of the fluvial processes of Shillong, it is necessary to understand how Shillong grew.

Shillong has grown as an enclave in the midst of rural society catering to the administrative and educational needs of the surrounding areas. In fact the process of urban growth of Shillong can be traced back to the period 1863-64 when the British shifted the headquarters of Khasi and Jaintia hills from Cherrapunjee to Shillong. The need for establishing a sanitorium for the European residence of Assam and district civil station was felt by Sir Rowlatt (Principal Assistant Commissioner). Thus Shillong was chosen as the station as it had a central location between Shylet plains in the south and Assam valley in the north.

In 1874 the British administration declared Shillong as the capital of Assam province which then had a population of about 1363 people. As Shillong was growing it was ncessary to acquire more land and the British administration through agreement with the Syiem of Mylliemm acquired more land which are now known as European ward, Police Bazar, Jail Road and present Cantonment as well as Lachumiere hill in perpetual lease.

It is seen then even in those days settlement sprung up in those areas of the present city which had a moderate slope and in areas which could be easily accessible. Thus the steep slope of Laban, Lumparing area inspite of being the earliest settlements in the area did not grow at a faster rate as the rest of area. It was only with the rise of population and the tremendous population pressure of land that these areas were encroached upon by urban functions.

In 1901 the total population of the township was 9621. In 1909 the Shillong Municipality was established which also included new areas of Laitumkhrah, Hoppinkson Estate, Malki, Mawprem, Laitkor forest.

The total population by 1911 was around 13639 showing an increase of about 41.16% per cent from the previous census.

The process of urbanization which was started by the British experienced a greater expansion after Independence in 1947 when a new thrust of horizontal expansion was experienced by Shillong due to large immigration from the then East Pakistan. Vacant land in Laitumkhrah, Laban, Malki etc. were occupied by the residential buildings. Proper planning in case of residential expansion was not done at that stage as settlements grew up on steep slopes and water divides by the side of the main lines of communication without paying much emphasis to the physiography of the area. This has had an adverse effect on the ecological balance of the city.

By 1951 Shillong urban area included both the municipality and the cantonment, which together recoreded a total population of 58512.

By 1961 the township of Nongthymmai and Mawlai had developed and formed two census town of the Shillong Urban Agglomeration. Due to the unrestricted residential expansion there were changes in the municipal boundary of the surrounding areas like Happy Valley, Umlyngka, Upper Shillong, Nongkseh, Lawsohtun, Madanriting, Pynthorumkhrah, Nongmynsong and Umpling, which also developed urban characterstics in their morphology.

In 1971 when the new state of Meghalaya was created Assam's capital was shifted to Dispur and Shillong automatically became the capital of Meghalaya with a total population of about 122752.

In 1981 census Shillong recorded a population of 174703, which increased to 222273 people by 1991 showing a growth rate of about 27.23 per cent from 1981-1991.

In view of the vast expansion of Shillong, the Urban Development Office, of the Government of Meghalaya, has identified a master plan, which includes the Shillong Urban Agglomeration and 32 villages in and around Shillong, and stretches from Barapani in the north to Mawlyngad in the south and Wah Umiam in the west to Tynring in the east.

An analysis of the slopes of Shillong reveals that there are mainly four categories of slope i.e. below 5°, 5°–10°, 10°–15°, above 15°; which can be grouped as gentle slope, moderate slope, moderately steep slope and steep slope. Frequency distribution of slope suggest that about 3.87 per cent of Shillong Master Plan area has gentle slope and is mostly observed in parts of Happy Valley, Pynthorumkhrah, Polo Ground. Around 40.65 per cent of the city is coverred by moderate slope including the central part of the city. Lawsohtun, Kenche's Trace, Bishnupur, Lumpering and Alugudam etc. area are covered by moderately steep slope and account for about 25.16 per cent of the total geographical area of the Shillong city. It is here in the moderately steep slope area where the loss of vegetation cover as a result of urban expansion has accelerated high run-off, which in turn has lead to soil loss and gully formation. The first and second order streams tend to dominate in these areas. Rill and gully erosion has been enhanced here, which in turn has promoted rock fall as there is no binding matrix. Nearly 6.45 per cent of the area has steep slope and covers larger parts of Mawlai, Mawprem and Madanriting.

Slope in turns determine the drainage of an area and the significance of drainage in the evolution of landscape has long fascinated the geomorphologists, hydrologists as well as geologist. Probably nothing epitomizes the history of a region's physiography as the history of a river. For rivers and valleys have a special place in the development of landforms, which made W.M. Davis remark that "landforms is the function of its structure, process and time" while discussing his normal cycle of erosion.

Shillong being situated in the humid tropical climatic region of the world, drainage tends to constitute one of the most important element of surface geodynamics.

In the absence of other agents it is post action and running water, which perhaps acts as the main agents of erosion in shaping the relief and the development of the present landscape found in and around Shillong city.

Shillong is drained by the rivers Umshyrpi and Umkhrah, which roughly determines the municipal boundary of the city. These two rivers join near Beadon and Bishop to form the Ro Ro a tributary to Wah Umiam which flows towards the north of Shillong.

A glance at the drainage map of Shillong shows that this area is dominated by lower order streams. Upper Shillong to the south-west and Laitkor to the south-east acts as a water divide where elevation is maximum. There are also quite a few river basins in the area. There are numerous nalas in the north and eastern part of the city which are actually the tributaries of the Umkhrah river, but some of them are now being filled up due to urban expansion as these lands are encroached upon by men.

The Umkhrah river starts as the Umling river from near about Umpling/Rynjah towards the southern side of the city. The Umkhrah river passes through the northern sector of Shillong, where as the Umshirpi follows a course towards the south.

On the course of the Umkhrah river towards the eastern section lies the Spread Eagle Falls. From Phudmawri, the Umkhrah takes a north-westerly direction and follows towards Beadon Bishop Falls.

The river Umshyrpi starts from the Crinolines Falls in the Lumpering area taking a north-westerly direction and joins the river Umkhrah near the Bishon Falls and Mawprem. The drainage pattern is sub-parallel to dendritic in nature as suggested by the drainage map of the area. The streams tend to follow the joints and faults of the area, which is reflected by almost straight stream course. The initial slope of the area, which is dominated by ridges and valley topography have also had its role in the drainage pattern.

An analysis of the drainage density shows that Shillong has moderate to high and very high density. A cursory look at the drainage map show that low density occurs in patches throughout the area. This may be due to constructional activities in certain areas, which have led to filling of the streams. However, the low density also indicate that these river basins are located at regions of highly permeable sub-soil with thick vegetational cover which should not be disturbed as the volume of run-off is governed primarily by infiltration characterstics which in turn is related with vegetation cover besides slope and soil type.

However, due to high rate of urbanisation, which exerts the pressure of population on land, the steep slope and water-sheds have been encroached upon by human activities and settlements. This has promoted indiscriminate felling of trees thereby reducing the percolation capacities.

Infact, it has been observed that during recent years at least seven spring in Laban, Lumparing, Lawshotun area and Upper Nongthymmai having an average slope of 15°–20° has dried up, perhaps because of the falling of trees due to constructional activities in their chatchment areas.

Again, the quality of water in the streams, are deteriorating and this deterioration is mainly because the streams are often used for dumping of waste and garbage. The plastic packets and other non-biodegradable products, which are thrown in large number poses serious threat to the streams. They not only pollute the water but also clog and block the stream flow, thereby hindering the natural flow of the streams e.g. stone quarries at Nongthymmai, Rynjah, Pynthorumkhrah, Mawlai, which are located on the banks of the Demthring and Wah Umkhrah have all added to the pollution of water. It has also led to siltation of the streams.

Atleast four public latrines are loacted by the side of the Umpling nala within 30 meters up-stream of the intake of Umpling water supply. All these have an adverse effect, on the quality of the drinking water of the city.

Again untreated sewage water has been allowed to flow along roadsides and open patches, which in turn mixes with the water of streams are tapped for drinking water. The capacity of natural channels to transport drainage water has often been reduced because of siltation, weeds and refuse resulting to serious ecological imbalance. Infact, most of the streams are disappearing under the impact of urbanization and demand for more areas under urban funcitons. This perhaps calls for a micro level study as to find out how the sterams of Shillong can be saved to play a greater role in the proper and planned development. It thus calls for a proper management of the streams in order to save the picturesque hill station of Shillong from ecological disastor.

To conclude the planners should restrict the indiscriminate felling of trees in the catchment areas of the streams so as to increase water discharge of the streams. Dumping of garbage on the banks should be banned. There is also the need for identification of an alternative site for stone quarries. Aforestation programmes should be inducted especially in the steep slopes. Filling up of streams leading to drying or seepage of water should also be discouraged.

9

RIVER UMIAM AND ITS ROLE IN HYDRO-ELECTRICITY GENERATION, TOURISM DEVELOPMENT AND INDUSTRIAL GROWTH

UTTAMA CHOUDHURY

When we talk of river as a resource, it appears to us as a great blessing. Its importance and usefulness can be traced back to the ancient times when most of the great civilization emerged in the river valleys. The rivers then provided the human community with the much needed water which has been rightly termed as the essence of life. With the passage of time, man gained more knowledge and a great advancement took place in civilization. Man, in fact became the master of nature. As a result, rivers – one of the important endowments of nature, came to be used and controlled by man for various purposes. Today, rivers serve as a source of irrigation, hydro power generation, navigation, etc. Besides, they present a beautiful spectacle which breathes into us an unmixed and untainted pleasure. Now, when we consider the North Eastern Region of India, immediately a picture comes into our mind representing the miniature form of the geographic macrocosm of the Indian subcontinent. The North East India with its seven sisters namely, Assam, Arunachal Pradesh, Meghalaya,

Mizoram, Manipur, Nagaland and Tripura has a total geographical area of 255,000 sq. kms and is drained by numerous big and small rivers such as the Brahmaputra, River Kameng, Subansiri, Dhansiri, Sionsang, Umiew and many others. River Umium is one such river which flows towards the north of Meghalaya and joins River Koili near Karbi Anglong (Mikir Hills) before flowing into the Brahmaputra. The water of this river orginates from the creeks and crevices of several hills located in the Umiam region which is located at a distance of about 16-17 kms from Shillong, the capital of Meghalaya. One of these hills is known as "U Lum Sohpet Bneng" in the local dialect which means the naval of heaven. A famous folklore is also associated with it. The hill is believed to connect the heaven and the earth and so the Khasis of this region claim to be of divine origin, the region with its river and the hils has a great cultural significance as well. The river flows over an area which comprises of the Archean formations of the Shillong Plateau and rocks like gneisis, schist, quarzite and conglomerates. The topography over which it flows is highly undulating and as such waterfalls have also developed in its course. Thylliej Lyngwa Falls and Shrem Falls are the two waterfalls on this river The geology as well as the physiography of the region largely controls the flow of this river and it forms a flat emabankment when it enters the plains. Besides, the Umiam Lake has made it all the more popular among the tourists and the anglers.

Objective

The main objective behind presenting this paper is to discuss the impact of River Umiam on the lives of the people of this region and the various dimensions of development that could be opened and widened due to this river. I also intend to discuss River Umiam in relation to hydro power generation, industrial growth and tourism development. The paper also intends to highlight those spheres in which remarkable success can be achieved if the river water is properly and judiciously utilised.

Methodology

The paper is based mainly on fact findings and necessary data and other facts have been collected from various published works which has been substantiated by some primary data as well obtained largely by observation. Some simple statistical techniques have also been adopted to present a comprehensive picture about the river's work in the development process.

Database

Data have ben collected from two sources : (1) Primary (2) Secondary.

Information regarding energy comsumption by industries and employment generation, etc. were obtained largely by observation and interviewing the people of this region, whereas facts about the river and hydro-electricity development, tourism developement, etc. have been gathered from various secondary soucrces like, the published works of Meghalaya Tourism Developemnt Corporation, Perfomarnce highlights issued by the Commerical Wing of the MeSEB, etc.

Hydro-Electricity Generation

When we talk about development related to a river, an important aspect which comes into our mind is the generation of hydro-electricity. River Umiam gained its popularity for its potentail of generating hydro-electricity. At present, it is the biggest power project in the State of Meghalaya. The Umiam Hydel Project was commissioned on 1st March, 1966 and after completion, it was subsequently transferred by ASEB to MeSEB on 21st January, 1975. The installed capacities of the different stages of the Umiam Project are :

Stages	**Installed Capacity**
Stage–I	36 MW
Stage–II	18 MW
Stage–III	60 MW
Stage–IV	60 MW
Total Installed Capacity	**185 MW**

Stage-V with an installed capacity of 2×30 MW has been explored over River Ungot, a tributary of River Umiam. The Umiam dam is the first high dam in the State which has been constructed in a highly seismic zone. The dam has two angles in its axis to meet the demands of a difficult topography and rock structure.

Total Energy Generated in the year 1995-96 by the Umiam Project

Umiam Stage-I	97.262 MWKH
Umiam Stage-II	45.716 MWKH
Umiam Stage-III	160.942 MWKH
Umiam Stage-IV	186.316 MWKH

This project came up largely because of the assistance extended by the American Govt's Agency for international development which provided 2.225 million dollars for this project and the Japanese Government which provided the much needed financial aid for the 4th turbine and the generating unit for the power station. Today, when the world is faced with problems of pollution and depletion of power resources, hydro-electricity can be a very easy and an effective solution to both these problems. It is in fact a nobel step towards solving the problem of global energy crisis due to the exhaustion of resources like coal and petroleum. Thus, River Umiam has proved to be a boon as hydro-power generated from this river is pollution free and does not impose any hazardous impact upn the regions envirionment. It also contributed to the industrialisation process and has opened some more new dimensions of development in this region.

Industrial Growth

The Industrial Area at Barapani developed because of many reasons but one important factor which needs special emphasis is the availability of cheap hydro-eletric power from the Umiam project. A number of industries were set up in this region but only two major industries are found to be operating here. These are the R.K.B Cements (Pvt. Limited) and the Umiam Calcinate Plant which are associate insdustries and the Rapsang Group of Industries. Both these industries largely depend on the Umiam Project for their power requirements. Every month approx. 1.30 thousand kilowatt of hydro-electricity from the Umiam Project is consumed by the Rapsang Group of Industries. Besides, the water of this river is also utilized for various industrial purposes. Thus, River Umiam had been instumental in setting up of industries in this region. This had widened the scope of employment for the local people as well as the ousiders in this secondary occupation.North-East India is lagging far behind from the country's mainstream in the field of industrialisation but it is largely endowed with hydro-power with potentials which is popularly known as "White Coal". If this potentiality is properly utilized then this region can surely come up as one of the industrial regions of the country. Especially for a state like Meghalaya, such an effort is a remarkable achievement.

Tourism

Another important aspect which needs special mention is tourism development. The big artificial lake created after the dam of river Umiam has become a great attraction for the tourists. The lake provides a panoramic view and a great picnic spot. Angling is a great sport over here and hundreds of people are often seen flocked together for angling. The Umiam Tourism Complex with the Lake Resort had come up as one of the best tourist spots in the State. Just adjacent to it in the Wildlife Park covering an area of ten hectares at the hillock called "Lum Nehru" (after our country's 1st Prime Minister). This park also has an orchidarium with 96 different species of orchids. The Umiam Lake Resort earlier had some water sports facility consisting of water scooters, speed boats and sail boats with a floating restaurant named "Flying Duck". It was India's first Floating Restaurant-cum-sports Duck made up of specially constructed fibre glass floats. But due to variuos reasons, some of the attractions and facilities are no longer available now. But if the Government, the private agencies and the local people take up the initiative of developing this region and restarting all these facilities once again, then no doubt, the Umiam region can come up as one of the country's major tourist spots and can help the state to earn a significnat amount of revenue. Its only after the creation of the big artificial lake from the River Umiam that it has been possible to develop it as a tourist centre.

Conclusion

The region has large potentials of development and the river is contributing greatly in speeding up the development process. Now-a-days, development can be achieved in various ways and here are my few suggestions which can augment their process further. If the Government takes up the task of purifying the water of Umiam reservoir then pisciculture can be started on a large scale which would generate income and employment as well. River Umiam flows through a number of villages where the primary occupation of the people is cultivation. Moreover, the river banks have fertile soil which can support rich agriculture if the river water is judiciously used for irrigation This will increase the food produciton and will help to feed the teeming population of the State. These days a number of settlements have also spring up in the region which is polluting the environment. Besides, the top soil is also being removed due to large scale deforestation .The Forest Developemnt Corporation of Meghalaya, can start afforestation programmes by planting trees at the Dam site and the river banks which will help in conserving the environment and prevent soil erosion also.

The surplus flow of river has been alreadly checked by the construction of dam which has stopped the flooding of the river embankments in the rainy season. This was indeed a great step ahead. Thus, the river has proved to be a boon in many ways and has significantly influenced the region's physical and cultural surrounding. Though much research and study has not been undertaken on this river and its various geographical aspects but I do hope that in the near future, scholars and students would come up with much more intensive studies and new ideas for the utilisation of the river's potentiality as it is an important resource by which the region's development can be speeded up.

REFERENCES

Gopal Krishnan, R. *"Meghalaya : Land and People"*.

Merwein, P.T., *Meghalaya Hand Book*, Third Edition, 1992.

Philomen, E.P., *Glimpses of Meghalaya*.

"Basic Facts of Meghalaya" issued by the Directorate of Information and Public Relations, Meghalaya.

Performance Highlights; Meghalaya State Electricity Board's Commerical Wing, 1996.

10

GEOMORPHOLOGICAL CHARACTERISTICS OF THE IMPHAL RIVER BASIN AND THEIR IMPACT ON DEVELOPMENT

M.K. BANDYOPADHYAY

The Imphal River Basin covers the central and southern parts of the State of Manipur. The total length of the river within the State is about 280 kilometres and the basin area about 6800 km^2. Four broad physiographic divisions may be identified in the basin viz., (i) The hills in the North, East, West and South, (ii) The foothill zone separating the hills from the plains, (iii) The plains in the central part, and (iv) The Loktak lake occupying the southern part of the plains.

The Imphal river have nine major tributaries orginating from the hills bordering the basin. The basin is elongated in a north south direction. Evidence indicate that the Loktak lake, once covering the whole of the plain area, at present occupies only about 270 km^2 in the southern part. The lake is shrinking fast because of deposition of sediments transported by the converging streams coming from different directions. The surrounding hills, which give rise to numerous large and small streams, are made up of semi-consolidated and un-consolidated rocks like sandstone, conglomerates, shale etc. In the northern part of the basin, especially in the Ukhrul district, however the rocks are mostly calcareous, which also do not offer resistance to erosion because of the wet environment. Heavy rainfall in the north and east during the summer monsoon causes rapid erosion in the hills and the sediments load is deposited in the foothill zones as alluvial fans and in the flood-plains as aluvium, while the rest of the load is deposited in the Loktak lake. The Loktak lake and the smaller lakes adjacent to it once formed a contiguous water surface covering the vast area, almost the whole of the present plain land. Of late, these areas have been separated from the main body of the wetland due to the deposition of sediment by natural processes as well as human interference such as construction of roads and settlement and conversion of wetland into paddy land.

Flood of moderate intensity are common in the plains, usually they occur twice in a year. Severe floods occur once in 10 years, while very severe floods once in 20 years. The most severe floods occur when very heavy rainfall takes place simultaneously in different parts of the basin and the water converge in the plains in a synchronous manner. River training for checking floods in Manipur has not yet been done properly and breaches in river embankment often follow heavy downpour in the hills and extension of settlement and agriculture at the cost of forest have been responsible for the rapid destruction of forests in the hills, intensification of the process of soil erosion and consequent deposition of sediment in the lake.

From the above study it is concluded that the hills around the central plain will be devoid off vegetation cover within a few decades at the existing rate of exploitation of the largest fresh water lake in the North East India which will dry up due to heavy siltation and ecological disaster will follow as a result of the decay of the vast wetland. The Loktak multi-purpose project, with a capacity of 105 kW of electricity and having seven giant pumps for lifting water for irrigation in the western sector of the plains, will cease to function. The Ithai Barrage at the southern outlet of the lake will have to be abandoned. The largest fishing project of the Manipur Government at Takmu (Loktak) will stop function also local fishermen will be out of occupation. Moreover, the production of Tapra natant (water plants locally known as Heikak) which is the only substitute for rice for the poor men of the plain will disappear.

In order to save the situation it is necessary to take up plans for controlling deforestation in the hills and the plains, checking Jhum cultivation in the hills and at the same time take massive programme of afforestation with the help of the Non-Governmental Organisation including the village communities. Extension of agricultural land at the cost of forest land should be discouraged and instead intensification of agriculture in the valley should be encouraged. This will surely lead to a decrease in the rate of erosion and extend the life of the lake. Finally, vigorous environmental awareness programme should be initiated by the Government with the help of the NGOs.

11

TRADITIONAL RICE VARIETIES OF BARAK VALLEY

An Under Utilised Germplasm for Sustainable Agricultural Development of Flood-Prone Areas

DHRUPAD CHAUDHURY and JIBENDU DATTA

INTRODUCTION

In the history of human civilisation, river valleys have played a significant role in shaping and determining the fortunes of innumerable cultures. A river system is an important determinant of the ecological function of all systems along its course, spanning the watersheds where it, together with its tributaries arise, to the estuary (or delta) where it drains into the sea. Minshall *et al.* (1985) provide an interesting review of the developments in stream ecosystem theory and present a succinct view of the importance of lotic systems in systems dynamics. All along, the river system constitutes a critical driving variable, determining the functioning of each component ecosystem that it links. The system, thus, directly affects the well-being of all inhabitants dwelling within its area of influence.

The functioning of ecosystem processes in fluvial aquatic and terrestrial systems are regulated by events both in the upstream as well as the catchment of the river. Productivity of various ecosystems in the valley is thus subject to changes in the catchment as well as the varioius ecosystems in the catchment as well as the drainage system that it supports. It is widely acknowledged now that inappropriate landuse in the catchment area results not only in localised ecosystem process disruption, but may also bring about intensified soil erosion (Rai and Sharma, 1998), which in turn gives rise to tremendously enhanced sediment load in rivers ultimately leading to downstream siltation, raised riverbeds and consequent flooding in the lower reaches. Indeed, the disastrous effects of floods and river sedimentation in Bangladesh have been attributed to inappropriate landuse and the resultant land degradation and soil erosion in the Himalayan region (Upreti, 1993). Although this assertion is contradictory to views expressed by Ives and Messerli (1989) and is contested in the absence of conclusive supportive evidence (Grosjean *et al.* 1995), a strong perception remains nonetheless, linking sedimentation and recurrent floods in Bangladesh to a direct highland-lowland interaction. Indeed, the emergence of sandbanks and nascent islands in the deltaic region of Bangladesh are thought to be a consequence of such interactions. Downstream settlements may therefore, be dramatically affected by human activites upstream, and thus, have a significant stake in the conservation and proper management of upstream catchment areas.

The effective translation of these stakeholders' claims into ecologically sound catchment management as a long-term solution to their recurrent problem is, however, non-existent as the claims are neither recognised nor given due credence in the trade-off between needs of local inhabitants of the catchment area and those downstream. In fact, the process of determining stakeholders to a particular resource (or resource base) is, as yet, unclear and a subject of intense debate (Borrini-Feyerabaend, 1996). Not surprising, therefore, recognition of stakeholder claims and translation into an unambiguous, clear policy, incorporating demands of all stakeholders and ensuring protection of their rights is yet to emerge in a form which is practically applicable. Such a situation leaves most stakeholders in particular those that are spatially far removed from the geographical area of concern such as the downstream inhabitants, with no control on matters relating to catchment management even though they bear the brunt of catchment misuse, except perhaps, through recourse to political pressures which in most cases are inept and ineffective. The consequence is regular disruptions in downstream ecosytem functioning, commonly witnessed in the form of recurrent floods, resulting in loss of life and property each year.

Under such circumstances, downstream inhabitants have no choice but to develop their own methods of coping with natural disruptions to the normal cycle of activities, including those caused by seasonal changes in the behaviour of the river system consequent to upstream event. The evolution of human societies has innumerable examples of communities harmonising lifestyles with their immediate surroundings in response to the demands of a harsh and dynamic environment. Such innovative adaptation, developed through generations of empirical experience are reflected in all facts of their livelihood pattern, including their agricultural activities. Thus, traditional agricultural practices, particularly the agricultral calendar as well as the crops grown, reflect the gradual induction of an ecological knowledge gathered through years of experience. The degreee of acuteness of this knowledge in perhaps, best reflected in the variety of crops that are grown and the tremendous variation in landraces within those crops, each tailored by nature to the subtle changes in micro-enviroment and habitate consequent to the cyclic distruptions, caused by the driving variables at the larger landscape level and carefully selected over generation by the inhabitants of the area.

For the rural communities of North East India, harmonising lifestyles and livelihood activities to the dynamics of their immediate environment has been a routine process of generations. North East India has a demanding physiography, being predominantly mountainous, except for the Brahmaputra and Barak Valleys. The Eastern Himalaya on the north, parts of the Arakan ranges to the east and the Meghalaya Plateau (including Karbi Along) to the south form the catchment of the Brahmaputra; in contrast, the uplands of North Cachar, western Manipur and northern Mizoram constitute the watershed of the Barak river. The inhabitant of both the valleys, historically, have been subjected to periodic disruptions of the river system in the form of annual floods, with varying degrees of intensity. Over the past few decades, however, the frequency and intensity of floods have assumed worrying dimensions and have become a cause of serious concern for both the government, as well as the inhabitants of the two valleys. Governemnt efforts at flood control have been enormously expensive but pathetically inadequate and ineffective, leaving the citizens to the mercy of annual, recurrent floods. To compound matters, government policies in both flood control as well as agricultural development have been inappropriate, inefficient and counter productive. The result has been ineffectual flood control measures which actually prolong the duration of waterlogging instead of ameliorating the situation (Agarwal and Narain, 1991) and the gradual erosion of traditional practices and agro-diversity which hitherto enhanced risk spreading for the farmers, ensuring a productivity at least at subsistence levels.

Floods in Barak Valley : A Brief Appraisal of the Scenario

The Barak Valley, comprising the administrative districts of Cāchar, Hailakandi and Karimganj, lies approximately between longitudes 92°13′ to 92°16′E and latitudes 24°08′ to 25°09′N. The valley forms the drainage basin of the river Barak and her numerous tributaries as they traverse the plains before entering Bangladesh, enroute to the Bay of Bengal. The valley, thus, is dissected by the numerous waterways besides being dotted by several waterbodies, locally known as Beels.

The Barak valley covers a total area of 6633.41 km^2 and as per the Census of 1991, has a total population of 24,91,496 of which an estimated 19 per cent of the total geographical area of the valley is under agricultural landuse, with 36 per cent constituting the net cropped area. About 9 per cent of the valley is flood prone, which translates to 19 per cent of gross cropped area. A summary of the agricultural landuse statistics is provided in Table 11.1; this also includes data on the total area under different cropping intensities in the three districts.

Table 11.1 : Basic Agricultural Landuse Statistics of the Barak Valley (in Hactares)

	Districts			
	Cachar	*Karimganj*	*Hailakandi*	*Total*
Geographical Area	3775532	153199	132610	663341
Gross Cropped Area	141301	102171	56945	300417
Net Cropped Area	115729	78876	44670	239275
Area Under				
Single Crop	84447	42811.5	28100	155358.5
Double Crop	48130	29679.5	9230	87309.5
Triple Crop	3128	812.5	300	4240.5
Dought Prone	3372	NA	NA	NA
Flood Prone	33336	23328	1050	57714

Source : Joint Director, South Assam, Department of Agriculture, Silchar.

A detailed account on the extent of flood prone areas in the three districts is additionally provided in Table 11.2. It is clear from Table 11.2 that while Hailakandi has the lowest flood prone area (1.84 per cent of the gross cropped area), large areas of the both Cachar and Karimganj districts are affected by floods, with the former having the largest proportion of arable land susceptible to annual submergence. An examination of the data for agricultural sub-divisions reveals, however, that Ramkrishnanagar sub-division in Karimganj district has the maximum arable land prone to floods and accounts for 61 per cent of the flood prone area in the district. In other words, an exceptionally high proportion of arable land of this sub-division is affected by floods in comparision to all its counterparts in the valley.

Table 11.2 : Extent of Flood Prone Areas in the Barak Valley

Districts	*Agricultural Sub-divisions*	*Flood Areas (in ha)*	*Total of the districts (in ha)*	*As % of the GC of the district*
Cachar	Silchar	18548		
	Sonai	14788		
	Lakhipur	NA	33336*	23.59*
Karimganj	Karimganj	9000		
	Ramkrishnanagar	14328	23328	22.83
Hailakandi	Hailakandi	1050	1050	1.84

(*excludes Lakhipur Sub-division)

Source : Joint Director, South Assam, Department of Agriculture, Silchar.

The intensity of damage caused by annual floods canot be ascertained by an examination of these figures alone. In order to fully appreciate the actual extent of damages caused by such annual disruptive events, a brief account is provided in the subsequent paragraphs and accompanying tables describing the impact of floods in the year 1998, with particular reference to the agricultural sector.

The Floods of 1998 : A Case Study

The extent of damage caused by the floods in 1998 to different categories of agricutural land is shown in Table 11.3. An examination of the figures makes it amply clear that while approximately 19 per cent of the flood prone area of Cachar district and 47 per cent of Karimganj district were affected, the magnitude of floods was more dramatic in the district of Hailakandi.

Table 11.3 : Extent and Types of Arable land affected by Floods in 1998 (in Hectare)

	Cachar	*Karimganj*	*Hailakandi*
Aus Seeding / Mainfield	447	NA	919.34
Sali Seeding / Seedbed	1347	NA	580.55
Sali Mainfield	—	NA	90.25
Vegetable Crops & Others	635	NA	124.89
Total	6459	11050.75	1715.03
As % of CGA	4.57	10.82	3.01
As % of Flood Prone Area	19.38	47.37	163.34

Source: Joint Director, South Assam, Department of Agriculture, Silchar.

An additional 665 hectares of arable land of the district, over and above the normal flood prone areas were affected, submerging a total of 1715 hectares of crop land. This increased the flood prone area of the district from 1.84 per cent to 3.01 per cent of the gross cropped area – an increase of 64 per cent. An area of 1009.59 hectares of Aus and Sali cropland were completely submerged while 581 hectares of Sali seedling and seedbeds were destroyed. Although the total average submerged was less than that in the districts of Cachar and Karimganj, a large portion of the cropped area of in the district of Hailakandi was inundated for the first time (Table 11.3).

The human dimension in this event remain unreflected in the account given above and therefore, a glimpse on this aspect is provided in Table 11.4. The table enumerates the number of farm families affected in different holding size categories. Although figures for Kaimganj district remain unavailable, it is clear from the data that in both the district of Cachar and Hailakandi, 95 per cent of the affected families were either small, or marginal farmers while only 5 per cent of the farms with large holdings were flood affected. The pattern is probably a reflection of the distribution of

Table 11.4 : Number of Farms Affected in each Holding Size Categories

	Cachar	*Karimganj*	*Hailakandi*
Farm Families affected			
(a) Big Farmers	898 (4.48)	NA	615 (5.16)
(b) Small Farmers	7546 (37.46)	NA	5363 (45)
(c) Marginal Farmers	11591 (57.85)	NA	5952 (50)
Total	20035	NA	11930

Note : Numbers within brackets indicate % of total farm families for the district in each category.

Source : Joint Director, South Assam, Department of Agriculture, Silchar.

farm holdings in the valley. Although statistics available on this aspect pertain to the district of Cachar alone, it suggests nonetheless, that the majority of farm holdings are predominantly marginal (75 %), with an area of 2.5 acres or less (Table 11.5). Small holdings (2.5 to 5.0 acres) constitute 20 per cent of the total farms in the district, while the rest are made up by large holdings of 5 acres or more. The pattern of affected farm families, thus, closely reflects the distribution pattern of farm holdings in the valley.

Although figures for crop losses due to the floods of 1998 are unavailable, estimates have been made to ascertain the intensity of losses in agricultural production. These estimates, based on yield statistics for the three cropping seasons, namely, *Sali, Aus* and *Boro*, from the various administrative blocks of Cachar district, are presented in Table 11.6. It is clear from the table that the floods of

Table 11.5 : Number of Farm Families under Different Holding Size Classes in the District of Cachar

Farm Holding Size	*Number of Farm Families*
Big (5 acres or more)	9338
Small (2.5 to 5 acres)	37356
Marginal (2.5 acres or less)	140094

Source : Joint Director, South Assam, Department of Agriculture, Silchar.

1998 caused an approximate loss of 8563 MT of paddy in the valley or about 4 per cent of the combined *Sali* and *Aus* production. Of this, around 144.4 MT of *Sali* crop was destroyed while the damage of *Aus* crops is estimated to be around 8418.29 MT, or about 46 per cent of *Aus* production in the valley. The comparatively lower volume of *Sali* crop damage is understandable, as *Sali* crops are sown only in June-July. In contrast, *Aus* crops are sown in March-April and harvested in July-August. It is not surprising, therefore, that the full force of the floods was spent on the *Aus* crop and a larger proportion of the damage to the latter was proportionately lower. The damage to the crops was compounded due to the long period of waterlogging. Under normal circumstances, with the cessation of rains, the flood water recede fairly rapidly unless the rains continue for a prolonged period in the watersheds. In 1998 however, in spite

Table 11.6 : Estimated Loss in Agricultural Production in Barak Valley Due to the Floods of 1998.

Cropping Season	*Area Affected (in ha)*	*Estimated Mean Yield (MT / ha)*	*Estimated Loss in Production (MT)*
Aus (Autumn)	5396.34	1.56 + 0.23 (n = 12)	8418.29
Sali (Winter)	90.25	1.60 + 0.32 (n = 12)	144.4

Note: Estimates based on figures provided by Joint Director, South Assam, Department of Agriculture, Silchar..

of the cessation of rains in the uplands, the level of flood waters could not recede as sluice gates facilitating their discharge were not opened for fear of spillage of the river waters into the fields. As a result, waterlogging was prolonged leading to complete damage of the *Aus* standing crops, a scenario projected by Agarwal and Narain in their treatise on floods in India and attributed to inappropriate and misguided flood control measures (Agarwal and Narain, 1991).

Lessons from the Aftermath : The Critical Realities

The statistics provided in the preceding tables poignantly depict the harsh realities of present-day life in fluvial flood plains such as the Barak Valley. Three important dimensions having serious long-term implications, clearly emerge out of the scenario that demand immediate consideration. The first pertains to the trend of increases in flood-affected areas. The data clearly shows an increasing extent of flood-affected arable lands, significantly in districts that hitherto had low susceptibility to damage from floodwaters. Interestingly, these areas are also in the lower course of the fluvial plains, suggesting perhaps, an increase in sediment deposition and a resultant elevation in the riverbed. Permanent constructions built as flood control measures, such as embankments, could also be equally responsible for prolonged waterlogging. The latter probably contribute to the situation by hindering the normal flow of receding floodwaters and thus delay backflows into the river during the process of flood recession. The obstructions, thus, could effectively result in the stagnation of retained water levels of which could rise with each subsequent rainfall and accompanying surface run-offs from the surrounding uplands, ultimately resulting in spillage of the impounded water into adjoining areas hitherto unaffected by floods. This situation could aggravate with incessant rains and the failure to open the sluice gates to allow discharge of the flood waters into the river, leading to inundation of fresh areas, ultimately resulting in an increase in the extent of flood affected areas.

It has to be simulataneously borne in mind that the landscape of the Barak valley is dotted with numerous *beels* of different shapes and sizes. These waterbodies, under normal circumstances, act as sinks for the surface run-off from surrounding areas as well as the river. The *beels* have been subjected to sedimentation from the rivers for decades (Hunter, 1879). With the increase in soil erosion in watersheds and the corresponding sediment load of the lotic systems, siltation of the *beels* have aggravated, raising their beds and reducing their holding capacity. Hindrance to the water flow due to construction of embankments have further compounded the situation by facilitating sedimentation, effectively reducing the capacity of the *beels* to act as sinks. Consequently, overflow from the rivers as well as the *beels* have increased progressively each year, ultimately contributing to an increased inundation.

Inflations in the extent of flood affected areas imply a corresponding increase in the number of families affected. The socio-economic attributes of affected families form the second dimension of this scenario. The impact of floods is predominantly borne by the small and marginal farmers. Loss in agricultural production due to annual disruptions such as flood further weakens the economic conditions of this group. For such farm families, already compromised by their socio-economic conditions, annual losses in agricultural production for even a single season have tremendous implications. The economic conditions of these families do not afford them any flexibility to absorb the shocks of losses in agricultural production. Prolonged waterlogging deprives them of the chance to replant a second time within the season and robs them of the agricultural production, implying a complete loss of income for the season. Often, such losses in real terms mean an increased burden of indebtness sometimes forcing the farmers to mortgage the subsequent seasons production in order to ensure enough food for the family's survival, thus irreversibly pushing them into further penury with repeated setbacks suffered each year, some of these families face an inevitable displacement and become uprooted from their lands, losing the only means of livelihood known to them. The subsequent recourse is a forced migration to nearby urban localities in search of a fresh means of livelihood and an unwilling transformation from a self-reliant farmer to an unnoticed, disendowed ecological refugee. This transformation completely compromises their ability for productive inputs to the local economy and thus, has far reaching implications both for agricultural, as well as economic developement of the region.

The third and final dimension in the scenario, decidedly the most profound, pertains to the abessive political voice of the small and marginal farmers. Unlike the larger farmers, small and marginal farmers have little effectural political representation either at the State or National levels. Their voices, consequently, are rarely heard as their is no meaningful assertion for the control of their stakes at the larger landspace level (which includes the catchment of the rivers which so dramatically affect their lives), or even their immediate local suroundings. Translated in terms of their day-to-day life, this abnegates any opportunity to ensure execution of management options in the catchment or their immediate environment that guarantee the protection of their basic interests from the adverse effects of annual disruptive forces such as floods and therefore, condemn such adscripts to a continuation of their daily drudgery. As a result, the cycle of floods, inundation and loss of production, income and property remain a grim reality for such impoverished groups, often resulting in ablation of some of the members of this community from their roots. Although the critique expressed above is admittedly adscitious, it merits serious deliberation at the relevant forum, especially at the level of policy planning. A dismissive attitude may prove acervative to the problems of the region and therefore, seriously hinder long-term sustainable development.

The Search for Solutions : The Case for Traditional Knowledge Base and Agrodiversity

The message that clearly emerges from the assessment is the urgent necessity for effective control by farming communities over factors that influence their immediate means of livelihood and survival. It is obvious that the protection of their stakes in the context of highland-lowland interactions cannnot be guaranteed under the existing conditions, given the absence of recognition of their rights in the larger arena (that encompasses catchment management) and the lack of a determined effectual polity to initiate action towards at least the acknowledgement of their stakes. The situation is no better in their immediate envrionment, either given the inadequcy and inappropriateness of existing flood control mechanisms. The only factor which seems within their control and over which they possess sufficient knoweldge is the choice of the agro-diversity and the germplasm that they own. Such self-reliance was historically expressed by these communities through the choice of their agricultural crops, both for subsistence and for generating cash income, and the knowledge concerning the appropriate use of these agro-resources.

Over the years, even this control has been threatened and gradually eroded, ironically, in the quest for agricultural development. In the pursuit for increased agricultural productivity, egged on by the deterministic philosophy (however unfounded and misplaced) of a patronising technocracy, more and more acreage under traditional landraces have been replaced by the High Yielding Varieties (HYV). The active promotion of the new varieties by extension agencies and the often overt coercive pressures of market forces have left the farmers with little choice but to opt for such new varieties despite the additional costs for fertilisers, pesticides, herbicides and irrigation, this gradual transformation has reduced the total acreage presently under traditional varieties to about 46 per cent of the gross cropped areas in the valley.

In the enthusiasm for agricultural development and enhanced production, government agencies actively encourage and strive for the homogenisation of crops. In this misguided rush, technological dependency increases progressively, bringing about a gradual alienation of the farmers from their traditional knowledge base and a silent erosion of their control over agricultural resources, that prove fatalistic in the long run (Shiva 1991; Choudhury 1998). The ultimate consequence is an impoverished agro-biodiversity, a discarded and disrespected raditional knowledge and a self-reliance that is gradually strangulated by the misplaced supremacy of technocratic determinism. For the farmer, this means the lack of options for crop insurance against the uncertainties of natural events and the inability of the introduced varieties to withstand disruptions caused by floods, droughts or pestilence. Effectively, the farmers find themselves in a situation where their once endogenous production system has suddenly been transformed into an axogenous one, depriving them of their confidence in ensuring a hitherto assured food and economic security.

The solutions lie in tailoring and steering the agricultural production system towards an endogenous character. It also requires restoration of a larger degree of dependence on resources that are wholly owned and controlled by the local farming community and of which they possess an adequate knowledge, gleaned through empirical experience, thereby increasing the degree of their self-confidence and self-reliance (Choudhury, 1998; Choudhury and Singh, 1988). Such a system, obviously, has to have a firm foundation on the indigenous knowledge base and traditional germplasm with an appropriate blend of modern scientific technologies.

The Untapped Assets : Knowledge Base and Germplasm of Traditional Landraces

The knowledge base and germplasm among the farmers of Barak Valley, in spite of the erosion consequent to agricultural transformation, is impressive. It is obvious from Table 11.7 that even present-day farmers posses a substantial knowledge about their traditional paddy landraces. It has to be mentioned here that the figures provided in the table are on the basis of a limited survey and therefore, the actual figures for the whole valley would be substantially larger. Statistics are no indicators of the qualitative aspect of variables; figures in the table fail to tell the story of the nature and depth of knowledge regarding minute aspects of each of these varieties – the micro-climatic, micro-habitat, pedological as well as nutritional requirements of these varieties and the micro-habitats best suited for optimal performance for each landrace form the substance of their knowledge base.

Consequently, farmers are aware about the performance of each landrace under a variety of situations. This depth in knowledge helps them to select the appropriate variety for a given micro-habitat and climatic regime for each cropping season and thus helps them in infusing a large degree of crop insurance against disruptions in the natural cycle. As evident from Table 11.7, the farmers have

Table 11.7 : Knowledge Base and Existing Germplasm of Paddy Landraces Among the Farmers of the Barak Valley

	Sali	*Aus*	*Boro*
Knowledge			
Total varieties	133	35	23
Introduced	14	15	7
Germplasm*	131	35	23
Flood Resistance	21	–	–
Pest Resistance**	50	2	5
HYV (introduced)	6	1	3

* *includes tradtional and introduced varieties.*
** *for stored grain pests only, damage levels less than 10% of the grain.*
Source : Primary Surveys.

a wide range of landraces to choose from, for which they still maintain the germplasm. Some of these varieties are specifically selected for their yield, or their ability to withstand natural stress such as floods, drought or pestilence. In contrast, the agricultural agencies offer a choice of only ten varieties for all seasons combined with the single ability of high yeilds.

The knowledge and germplasm of the agrarian communities have been the basis of scientific efforts in crop improvement, whether in paddy or other crops. Even the much acclaimed high yeilding varieties have their origin in some humble, obscure traditional landraces. New nomenclatures disguise the origin of the improved variety and the false supremacy of the plantbreeder mask the contribution of the traditional farmers in selecting and developing these new agricultural "wonders". What the farmers fail to retain in the new varieties in thier quest for enhanced yields, is the inherent ecological plasticity to a large amplitude of stress conditions, thus, rendering the variety susceptible to even slight disruptions. This singular fact abnegates risk spreading and limits all the advantages gained from enhanced productivity — a fact foremost in the mind of traditional breeders while selecting their germplasm and therefore, more tolerant to variations in nature.

Risk spreading as a strategy towards crop insurance against natural disruptions and the resultant loss in production is a basic prerogative of traditional agricultural practices. In contrast, the government and extension agencies put more confidence on performances of a few select varieties. This is evident from Table 11.8 which lists the range of varieties recommended for cultivation during the different cropping seasons in Barak Valley by both farmers and extension agencies. The table is a summary of a sample survey and gives only an indication of the true picture. It suficiently demonstrates however, the larger range recommended by farmers in comparison to government agencies.

The wide choice available in traditional landraces for specific situations in nowhere more poignantly demonstrated than in the options for flood resistant varieties. While the choice in traditional varieties range to at least twenty one landraces, drawn from two generic groups, the *Asra* and *Badaal*, the government agencies recommend only two, that too, from traditional landraces. Initial evaluation trails are in progress on two more varieties as demonstrated in Table 11.9. The *Asra* landraces, incidently, are known to tolerate floodwaters to heights of over a metre and a half.

Productivity figures for the traditional paddy landraces are furnished in Table 11.10. These figures are for all the three cropping seasons for the three districts of valley. The figures give an idea of the productivity of traditonal varieties for the different seasons. Although this may not be comparable to the productivity of high yielding varieties, it is enough to provide a basic food security at subsistence levels. A simple estimate, based on the yield data averaged for all seasons, suggests that if the total flood prone areas of Barak valley were to be brought under traditional varieities, the annual production would stand at 100422.36 MT, or 3.04 per cent of the State's annual pady production (3, 3612.1×10^3 tonne, NEC Basic Statistics Handbook, 1995) and thus may afford some succour from the annual losses due to the floods.

The exercise to bring the floodprone arable areas under traditional varieties is obviously, not as simple as it seems. A serious strategy has to be evolved, involving agricultural scientists and technocrats from related disciplines, for selection and through evaluation of the suitability and performance of different triaditional landraces, before appropriate varieties suited to specific micro-habitat conditions and with sufficient ecological plasticity can be

Table 11.8 : List of Paddy Varieties Grown by the Farmers (Traditional) and Recommended by Government Agencies (Introduced) for the Different Cropping Seasons

Sali (winter paddy)		*Aus (autumn paddy)*		*Boro (summer paddy)*	
Sowing	June/July		Mar/Apr.		Nov/ Dec
Harvesting	Nov/Dec		Jul/Aug		Apr/May
Growth period	120/160 days		90/120 days		170/190 days
Traditional	Introduced	Traditional	Introduced	Traditional	Introduced
Badaal	Cauvery	Kachalaothi	Cauvery	Banglami	Cultivar I
Balam	Jaya	Kaimurali	IR 36	Boro I	IR 8
Biroin	Masuri	Munshimurali	Jaya	Boro II'	Krishna
Chaiyamora	Monohrsheil		Krishna		
Chotto-chaimora	Pankaj		Saket-4		
Dumsheil					
Harinarayan					
Kalijeera					
Najira					
Sahebsheil					
(10)	(5)	(3)	(5)	(3)	(3)

Source : Joint Director, South Assam, Department of Agriculture, Silchar and primary sample survey of selected farmers from Karimganj and Hailakandi districts

Table 11.9 : Flood Resistant Varieties Recommended by Farmers and Government Agencies for Cultivation in Barak Valley

*Traditional**	*Recommended***	*Introduces****
Asra : Amun, Bali, Badaal, Bhuttu, Dum, Goda, Koi, Lakshmi, Mainpuri, Moti, Paninoli, Sona, Suknil, Uba	Sheil Badaal Dhola Badaal	IET 11896 IET 11910
Badaal : Dhola, Goda, Hansh, Kacha, Methiman, Pende, Sheil		
(21 Varieties)	(2 Varieties)	(2 Varieties)

* Farmers' recommendations.

** Governement agencies.

*** Initial Evaluaiton Trail.

Source : Joint Director (South Assam), Department of Agriculture, Silchar.

Table 11.10 : Productivity of Traditional Paddy Varieties in the Barak Valley

	Sali	*Aus*	*Boro*
Area under cultivation	115199 (84)	10471 (7.64)	11430 (8.34)
Production (MT)	2016314 (85)	1848.8 (7.75)	18483.1 (7.75)
Yield (MT)	1.75	1.77	1.62

Note : Figures in brackets indicate percentage of total for all three seasons.
Source : Estimate based on figures provided by the Jt. Director, South Assam, Dept. of Agriculture, Silchar.

recommended for the purpose. Such exercises have been the fundamental mandate of agricultural universities and research organisations throughout the country and abroad. However, the lacking in their efforts has been the failure to provide location specific solutions, a consequence of the singleminded approach for high productivity and the subsequent drive for homogenisation. Such programmes of the government, therefore, can draw profitably from the experience of the local farming community. given a strong foundation in tradtional knowledge, a strategy can emerge which afford a much higher degree of crop insurance to the farmers against disruptive event such as floods and other natural disasters and in the process, take the farmers closer to a more secure food and economic endowment.

Conclusions

"...... Scientists and technologists are in turn taken to be that sociological category formally trained in Western science and technology, either in institutions in the West, or in Asian institutions Mimicking the paradigms of the West .... Development in this view is taken as synonymous with the introduction of Western Science and Technology in non-Western contexts" (Shiva, 1991).

The global legacy that colonial powers have left behind in their wake is the unflinching trust in western paradigms and thinking, be it in the realms of technology or economics. The singular victim in the process has been the indigenous knowledge systems of numerous nationalities throughout the erstwhile colonial world. As pointed out by Shiva (1991), the introduciton of ecological and economically inapproriate science and technology has led to under-development instead of development. Inappropriate technologies and misplaced economic paradigms reduce self-reliant communities to marginalised conditions. Unless this basic fact is acknowledged by our intelligentsia, policy-planners and administrators and a healthy respect for the traditional knowledge and practices reposed, the fate of communities such as the farmers of Barak Valley remain condemned to that of marginalisation, impoverishment and disendowment. A renewed confidence in the indigenous knowledge and practices of local communities with judicious infusions of appropriate, modern science and technological interventions to strengthen traditional technologies and practices needs to be the fundamental basis of future planning processes in order to guarantee food and economic security for the rural poor of the country. The introduction of traditional landraces in floodprone areas of the Barak valley, based on the knowledge and germplasm of the local communities, offers an excellent opportunity for such innovative approaches to development.

Acknowledgements

The authors are grateful to the various officials in the office of the Joint Director of Agriculture (South Assam), Government of Assam, Silchar who have been extremely cooperative in providing relevant figures and statistics. The paper could not have been possible without the help and ready cooperation of numerous farmers; the authors appreciate their help and ready hospitality. In fact, the paper is theirs'. We also thank the Head, Department of Life Sciences, Assam University, Silchar and the Principal, Moinaul Haque Choudhury College of Science and Technnology, Pachgram for providing the necessary facilities.

REFERENCES

Agarwal, A. and Narin, S. (Eds) (1991), *Floods. Flood Plains and Environmental Myths*. State of India's Enviroment 3. Centre for Science and Environment, New Delhi.

Borrini-Feyerabend, G. (1996), *Collaborative Management of Protected Areas : Tailoring the Approach to the Context.* Issues in Social Policy, IUCN, Gland (Switzerland).

Choudhury, D. (1998), Conserving Genetic Heterogeneity in North-East India: Indigenous Knowledge Systems and Opportunities for Sustainable Development. In : M.K. Raha and A.K. Ghosh (Eds) *North-East India : The Human Interface.* Gyan Publishing House, New Dehlhi. pp. 147-161.

Choudhury, D. Singh, Th. S. (1998), Agrosystems of North East India : Indices of Sustainability. In : R.C. Sundriyal, Uma Shankar and T.C. Upreti (Eds) *Perspectives for Planning and Development in North East India.* Bishen Singh Mahendra Pal Singh, Dehradun. pp. 64-68.

Grosjean, M., Hofer, Th, Liechti, R, Messerli, B, Weingartner, R. and Zumstein, S., (1995), Sediments and Soils in the Floodplains of Bangladesh : Looking up to the Himalayas. In : H. Schrier, P.B. Shah and S. Brown (Eds) *Challenges in Mountain Resource Management in Nepal. Processes, Trends and Dynamics in Middle Mountain Watersheds.* ICIMOD/IDRC/UBC. pp. 25-32. Hunter, W.W., 1879 *A Statistical Account of Assam. Vol. II* Trubner and Company, London and B.R. Publishing Corporation, New Delhi (Reprint, 1975).

Ives, J.D. and Messerli, B. (1989), *The Himalayan Dilemma. Reconciling Development and Conservation,* Routledge /UNU, London, New York.

Minshall, G.W., Commins, K.W., Petersen, R.C., Cushing, C.E. Burns, D.A., Sedell, J.R. and Vannote, R.L. (1985), Developments in Stream Ecosystem Theory. *Canadian Journal of Fishery and Aquatic Sciences* 42 : 1045-1055.

Rai, S.C. and Sharma, E. (1998), Comparative assessment of runoff characterstics under different land use patterns within a Himalayan watershed. *Hydrological Processes* 12 : 2235-2248.

Shiva, V. (1991) *The Violence of the Green Revolution.* Third World Network, Penang and Natraj Publications, Dehradun.

12

NORTH BENGAL RIVERS
Behavioural Pattern and their Impact on Development

M.M. JANA

North Bengal, located in the northern part of the state of West Bengal covers an area of about 21,625 km^2 of which 12 per cent are covered by hills, mountains and ridges and remaining 88 per cent are flat plains. The general slope is from north to south. The highest point is about 3,000 m in the north and the lowest point is about 50 m in the south. The region is intersected by numerous streams, rivers and rivulets. All their source region is in the Darjeeling Himalaya in the north. The rivers draining the North Bengal are : (i) Snow fed, (ii) rainfed, and (iii) the major rivers of North Bengal observed from the Satellite imageries is that they undergo drainage inversion from covering drainage in the hills to divergent drainage in the plains. Most of the rivers drain considerable amount of water during rainy season due to their large catchment area in the hills. All rivers carry huge amount of sediment loads with water at that time due to high rate of soil erosion in the hills of various reasons. As most of the rivers have high gradient and huge amount of water they carry so they are potentially rich in production of hydro-electricity. A few hydro-electric projects were installed in the hilly parts of these rivers. Moreover, these rivers are divided into (i) high run-off zone, (ii) high infiltration zone, and (iii) recharge zone. Floods are common in North Bengal rivers. Reasons for frequent floods are excessive rains in a short duration, large catchment area of rivers, snowmelt water, low carrying capacity of rivers due to high siltation in the river beds. The rivers had changed their courses due to sudden bursting of artificial water storage by landslides and bank erosion. Recent floods in North Bengal are significant in the sense that they gave clear indication about the negligence of river management and development.

High deforestation in the hills and ridges leads to landslides and soil erosion. The hills of Darjeeling Himalayas, have been highly deforested and degraded due to human interference. In the past, the forests in the hills were cleared for tea plantation. Terrace cultivation was started in the hills for production of crops and the remaining forests could not withstand the threat of the increasing population which was due to high rate of immigration from other states or countries at different times. As a result, high rate of soil erosion is the characteristic feature of the hill areas of Darjeeling. The drainage system of the Himalayan rivers debauching into the plains acquire a typical characteristics of the respective basins. All these rivers with their upper catchments in the hills have funnel shaped basins with narrow outlets at the foothills. The upper reaches are underlain by geologically weak formation of highly sheered and closely jointed rocks of exfoliated mica-schists and mica-gneisses and schists. The lithological contact is well presumed and has a direct bearing on the gradient of the long profile of the rivers. In the plains, the gradient of the rivers falls significantly and the rivers suddenly widen. Under these conditions, the rivers adjust themselves by changing their processes from erosional to depositional to meet with the new hydrological requirements induced by the change of gradient. Rivers attain braided channel which further widen with lateral erosion of the non-cohesive bank. As a result, new channel is formed. Shifting of the channels and abandoning the existing ones are most common in the rivers of North Bengal. With little topographical variations in the lower reaches, overflowing of water of one river causes flood in the catchment area of the other river. In many places, bank erosion are very difficult to trace out. The construction of longitudinal embankments along the rivers has increased the rate of rise of the bed level. Unable to spill over, the excess sediments were deposited in many places of the river-beds. The problem is accelerated due to careless diversion of water from rivers for irrigation and domestic uses. As a result, discharge decreases and the rivers become incompetent to carry the silts and debris. Breaching of embankments, removal of boulders by the people and theft of wireguards from the embankments weaken the structure which easily give way to any significant increase in the discharge of the rivers in the peak season. Extraction of gravels created depression adjacent to the bank into which the water is found to be diverted during the high flow of water in the monsoon months. These activities cause severe bank erosion and consequently inundate adjoining areas of the rivers.

The drainage system is very poor and stagnation of water is a common phenomenon in the region even after the flood has receded. Scarcity of suitable lands for habitation have compelled the lowland dwellers to construction their permanent houses in the low lying areas either on the river beds or on sides of banks because entire highlands are devoted to cultivation of various crops. New settlers, with very little knowledge about the erractic nature of North Bengal rivers occupy every tract of waste lands that are generally, the beds of old or abandoned channels. Much of the serious problems associated with floods and flooding are attributed to the fact that man and rivers can not be overlooked and they are interrelated with each other. Management and planning are urgently necessary to control the flood and soil erosion so that the region can be protected from frequent floods and damages.

ANNEXURE : BRIEF NOTES

WATER RESOURCE MANAGEMENT IN BRAHMAPUTRA VALLEY

Jaysree Borah

The river system of Brahmaputra valley, though snow feed, are dependent upon the monsoon, for their peak flow. With the variations of monsoon, their discharge also varies greatly from time to time. Recently new problems have been added by deforestation, unplanned utilization of land, shifting cultivation, soil erosion, etc. Consequently water resource plannning in the context of our agricultural economy becomes extremely imortant. In this paper an attempt will be made to study the potential water resources of Brahmaputra valley, its proper utilization and management for overall development of the region. Here some measures like soil reclamation, flood control, afforestation, scientific landuse, etc, will aslo be discussed for an understanding of a proper management of water resources of Brahmaputra.

RELEVANCE OF ENVIRONMENTAL ASPECTS IN RIVER VALLEY AND WET LAND DEVELOPMENT PROJECTS : ISSUES AND APPROACHES TO SUSTAINABILITY

V.T. Darlong

Rivers and riverine system continues to play vital role in the progress and development of human civilization. Consequently, the human impact on the riverine system and its water is as old as the human civilization itself. This impact is clearly visible in the deliberate modification of rivers and water bodies, as well as through increasing pressure of riverine system and water as units of development activities in the form of creation of dam for hydel power generation, irrigation, water supply, industrial usage and so on. Here lies the relevance of environmental aspects in the use and development of river system for long-term sustainability and conservation.

Although environmental aspects have been generally well accepted in the most planning and development exercises, debate continues as to the priorities of environmental issues to be considered particularly in the context of water resource development in fragile mountainous areas like North East India. Integration of environmental aspects beyond the boundaries of interdepartmental functionings also continues to be a dilemma, much as integration is yet to be achieved to desired degree. This is perhaps due to lack of proper understanding of environmental aspects in water resource development of riverine system.

The present paper attempts to illustrate the relevance of environmental aspects of water resource development by consdiering various issues of environment that need to be addressed in the context of fragile mountain systems of North East India and socio-cultural and economic dependency of diverse communities of the region on its river system. Current approaches to sustainable and equitable use of such resources as a way of reconciling environment and development are also briefly discussed.

STRATEGIES FOR DEVELOPMENT OF THE GABHARU RIVER BASIN IN NORTH EAST INDIA

L. Roy & A.K. Bora

River basin represents a well defined areal unit drained by a river system. Assuming importance as a fundamental geomorphic unit, it provides a physical basis for integrated management and development of its land and water resources.

This paper makes an attempt to suggest strategies for the development of the Gabharu river basin, one of the important river basins of the Brahmaputra river system in India's North East.

Considering the physical bases and resource potentialities of the geomorphic units of the basin delineated through visual interpretaion of satellite imagery, an attempt has been made to accord priority to each of these units for initiating developmental strategies. Finally an environmentally sound development planning for the basin is suggested.

INDEX